COLLECTIVE CARE

Collective Care

Indigenous Motherhood, Family, and HIV/AIDS

Pamela J. Downe

TC▸ TEACHING CULTURE

UNIVERSITY OF TORONTO PRESS

Toronto Buffalo London

Toronto Buffalo London
utorontopress.com
Printed in Canada

ISBN 978-1-4875-8764-2 (cloth)
ISBN 978-1-4875-8763-5 (paper)
ISBN 978-1-4875-8765-9 (EPUB)
ISBN 978-1-4875-8766-6 (PDF)

Library and Archives Canada Cataloguing in Publication

Title: Collective care : Indigenous motherhood, family, and HIV/AIDS / Pamela J. Downe.
Names: Downe, Pamela, 1964– author.
Series: Teaching culture.
Description: Series statement: Teaching culture: UTP ethnographies for the classroom | Includes bibliographical references and index.
Identifiers: Canadiana (print) 20200341901 | Canadiana (ebook) 2020034224X | ISBN 9781487587642 (hardcover) | ISBN 9781487587635 (softcover) | ISBN 9781487587659 (EPUB) | ISBN 9781487587666 (PDF)
Subjects: LCSH: HIV-positive women – Saskatchewan – Social conditions – Case studies. | LCSH: HIV-positive persons – Saskatchewan – Social conditions – Case studies. | LCSH: Indigenous women – Health – Saskatchewan – Case studies. | LCSH: Mothers – Health – Saskatchewan – Case studies. | LCSH: HIV infections – Social aspects – Saskatchewan – Case studies. | LCSH: Health planning – Saskatchewan – Case studies. | LCSH: Social medicine – Saskatchewan – Case studies.
Classification: LCC RA643.86.C22 S23 2021 | DDC 614.5/993920082097124 – dc23

We welcome comments and suggestions regarding any aspect of our publications – please feel free to contact us at news@utorontopress.com or visit us at utorontopress.com.

University of Toronto Press acknowledges the financial assistance to its publishing program of the Canada Council for the Arts and the Ontario Arts Council, an agency of the Government of Ontario.

Canada Council for the Arts
Conseil des Arts du Canada

ONTARIO ARTS COUNCIL
CONSEIL DES ARTS DE L'ONTARIO
an Ontario government agency
un organisme du gouvernement de l'Ontario

Funded by the Government of Canada
Financé par le gouvernement du Canada
Canada

Contents

Preface

Journalist Sonia Shah (2016, 8) quotes UCLA infectious disease expert Brad Spellberg: "You hear that we have to win the war against microbes. Really? They are so numerous that they outweigh us by one-hundred-thousand fold. Win the war? I don't think so." Medical anthropologists and public health scientists are often called on to speak publicly about global health wars and victories. COVID-19, Ebola, Zika, and monkeypox are recent headline-grabbing outbreaks, as is the resurgence of measles, bubonic plague, and polio. These epidemics are emerging alongside one of the deadliest and longest pandemics in human history: human immunodeficiency virus and acquired immunodeficiency syndrome (HIV/AIDS). The World Health Organization estimates that since HIV was first identified in the early 1980s, some seventy million people have been infected with it, and thirty-five million have died from HIV/AIDS-related causes.

There are families affected by every one of these infections and deaths. Except for some groundbreaking studies – see Hunleth (2017) and Block and McGrath (2019) – there is not much known about these families. This book addresses this lack by exploring the family dimensions of the HIV/AIDS epidemic on the Canadian prairies, working in partnership with Indigenous mothers. The ethnographic story that unfolds in the coming chapters is one of HIV-related suffering and stigma as well as community strength. It is grounded in the local context of central and northern Saskatchewan, Canada. However, given that Canada's colonial history of hostility towards Indigenous Peoples is one that is shared by peoples of other colonized lands, and that Saskatchewan has drawn national and global attention for having HIV/AIDS rates on par with Rwanda and Nigeria, this local story has global relevance.

I advance the central argument that despite the idealized models of individual motherhood that dominate this neoliberal moment in North American society, collective care is the cultural touchstone for Indigenous mothers and their families living with, and affected by, HIV/AIDS. Collective mothering, however, draws harsh criticism from individual service providers, teachers, and law enforcement officers, as well as the broader public. Accusations of irresponsibility, inability, and a lack of maternal love are commonly made. Still, the ethic for collective care endures in spite of such criticism, providing support in times of duress and ill health. Thirty women and twenty-three men invested their time, trust, and stories in the project on which this book is based. They consistently and clearly claimed that raising healthy, resilient, responsible, and proud children requires a network of kin – "a mom team" as one participant called it.

Conducting anthropological research and writing a book also requires a team, and I will be forever grateful to those who contributed to this work. First and absolutely foremost, I thank AIDS Saskatoon staff and the people who access their services. This agency does heroic work. There is great loyalty to the agency among the people who access its services, and deservedly so. In my fifteen years of partnership with AIDS Saskatoon, we have completed five projects and I have had the pleasure of working with Jason Mercredi, Natalie Kallio, Cheryl Antoine, Christine Bennett, Erin Beckwell, and Heather Byrne. I owe particular thanks to the staff members who were directly involved in formulating and conducting the research on which this book is based: Gina McKay, Nicole White, Duane Minish, Cathy Johnson, Megan Morman, Andrea Kotlar-Livingston, and – above all – Sherri Doell and Eleanor Prosper. The members of the Community Advisory Board who represented fourteen organizations that provide Indigenous and health services to those affected by HIV/AIDS offered invaluable insight and guidance. Special gratitude is owed to Janine Cardinal for her wisdom, guidance, and fearlessness. I cannot identify the research participants by name, and pseudonyms are used throughout this book; however, nothing here would be possible without their trust, enthusiasm, and ongoing input. Any royalties from the sale of this book will go to AIDS Saskatoon to support all that they do. Thank you, all.

Second, I want to recognize that the research on which this book is based was supported by a grant from the Canadian Institutes for Health Research, as well as funding from the National Network of Aboriginal Health.

Third, I am extremely appreciative of my academic collaborators and colleagues who contributed to and supported this research. The core research team consisted of University of Saskatchewan colleagues and friends Sylvia Abonyi (Community Health and Epidemiology), Karen Lawson (Psychology), and Jennifer Poudrier (Sociology). It has been a privilege to work with some stellar students on this project: Katherine Shwetz, Sarah York, Zachari Logan, Jody Shynkaruk, Melanie Bayly, Mitchell Anderson, Rachael Lammie, Mika Rathwell, Andrea Epp, Morgan McAllister, and Rebecca Dravland. I am very grateful to Debbie Croteau, the administrative assistant in the Department of Archaeology and Anthropology, for her assistance in administering the financial aspects of this work. The Department of Anthropology at the University of California (Los Angeles) was my home away from home in 2005 and 2010 when I was fortunate to hold visiting scholar status there. The interest in and feedback on my work from UCLA's Linda Garro, Carole Browner, Jason Throop, and all the students associated with the Mind, Medicine, and Culture seminar, as well as the Center for Everyday Lives of Families (CELF), were invaluable. I also want to express my deepest thanks to my colleagues, graduate students, and friends who were not directly involved in this project but who nevertheless supported it by attending fundraisers, public presentations, AIDS Saskatoon events; and by providing advice, feedback, and support when I needed it most: Angela Lieverse, Margaret Kennedy, Colleen Dell, Christine Chang, Jim Handy, Annette Desmarais, Linda McMullen, Allison Muri, Ray Stephanson, Ron Cooley, Clint Westman, David Bennett, Samantha Moore, Adrienne Ratuschniak, Janice Graham, Robin Whitaker, Michel Bouchard, Peter Stephenson, Susan Frohlick, Penny VanEsterik, and Jamil Sawaya.

I extend my deepest gratitude to the editorial team at the University of Toronto Press. Thank you to Carli Hansen, Anne Brackenbury, and John Barker for your hard work, enthusiasm, constructive feedback, and – most of all – your patience. I am extremely grateful to Terry Teskey, whose copy-editing strengthened this work, and to managing editor Robin Studniberg, for taking the lead in the final publication process.

Lastly, I am forever indebted to my home team. My husband, Jim Waldram, sustained me through all stages of this project and was my very best critic, as well as champion. It is an honour to share a life with such a supportive partner, devoted father, and acclaimed scholar. Thank you to our daughters, Kaitlin and Amara, for allowing me to experience motherhood, for their patience, and for bringing four amazing grandchildren into our lives. My sister, Kathryn Downe, and brother-in-law, Douglas Watling, were the first to read earlier drafts of this book. Their insights, feedback, and editorial assistance made me a better writer and scholar. More than that, their dedication to social justice, public education, and family has motivated me in all my professional as well as personal undertakings. Thank you to our Ottawa family – Virginia Caputo, Stefan Janhager, Melinda, and Alexander – for providing much-needed respites from work and reminding me of the restorative power of music, laughter, and friendship. Final acknowledgement goes to those who were here at the beginning of this project but not at the end: my mother, Evelyn Downe; my aunt, Cynthia Downe; and our dear Lucy Lynne. I am so grateful for everyone's love, kindness, and collective care. This book is for you, my family.

1

Opening

> There is a parable about a health care worker.... Standing on a riverbank she sees a few bodies floating by. She quickly sounds an alert and begins pulling the bodies out of the river. She applies first aid and resuscitates one person, but as soon as she looks up there are more bodies coming down the river. She and her companions are soon exhausted.... Then it occurs to them to look upstream to see what on earth is pushing the bodies in.
>
> *– Cathy Crowe (2007, 8)*

"Over thirty-three million? That's a big number," Dennis exclaimed. "I'm one of a whole lot of people fighting this thing!" We were talking about the worldwide rates of human immunodeficiency virus (HIV) and acquired immunodeficiency syndrome (AIDS). He was interested in discussing how his struggles as an Indigenous man living with HIV/AIDS in what has been described as Canada's "HIV hotspot" were situated in the global landscape of the pandemic. I did my best to recall the worldwide statistics from that year's *AIDS Epidemic Update* (2008) issued by the United Nations and World Health Organization. Rates of newly diagnosed infections had decreased slightly, but the profile was changing. More women were being infected than ever before. Although global AIDS mortality rates were also declining, death rates from AIDS-related tuberculosis were up, especially in children under the age of fifteen. "We got to work on this," Dennis said. I agreed.

Dennis and I first met shortly after AIDS Saskatoon – the primary HIV-related service provider in central and northern Saskatchewan, Canada – relocated from a small office space in a strip mall to a house with a large drop-in area just north of Saskatoon's downtown core neighbourhood. Dennis was one of the roughly 150 people who access services (hereafter referred to as PWAS) at AIDS Saskatoon every day. He was also the PWAS representative on the agency's advisory board. Gina McKay, the education and prevention coordinator at the time, had asked me to come to their new office space to meet with other staff, as well as Dennis. The shift in location had led to a shift in the PWAS. More women and children were accessing their services. With a much larger building, more services could be provided, including laundry facilities, computer stations, a donated clothes area, regular nutritious meals, a needle exchange, and a drop-in centre with comfortable furniture, hot coffee, and cable TV. "We are used to serving the men who come into our offices," Gina explained, "but the new location brings in a lot of women, children, and whole families. We want to serve them well, too." Dennis was eager to move forward with a project that focuses on families. "We need to do right by the mothers and families who are coming here. And it's not only important to us just here," he said, referring back to our earlier conversation, "it's a big world issue."

We tackled this "big world issue" over the coming decade. A Community Advisory Committee (CAC) was established with representatives from fourteen Indigenous and health-focused social service agencies and organizations in central and northern Saskatchewan. Dennis was one of two representatives of the PWAS at AIDS Saskatoon and the Saskatoon Area Network of Drug Users (SANDU). After two meetings with the CAC, it was clear that we all shared a desire and need to know more about the daily lives of mothers who live with, or are at risk for, HIV/AIDS. Our general discussions regarding families always circled back to discussions about mothers and motherhood. Our considerations of what services might best benefit HIV/AIDS-affected families always concluded with questions about maternal well-being. We ultimately developed a central and overarching question that would address what we needed to know: *What does it mean to be a mother in the context of HIV/AIDS?*

We hoped to learn the ways in which HIV/AIDS infection and risk affected motherly care, and how mothering affected women's experiences with HIV/AIDS. As well, we hoped to identify how AIDS Saskatoon and all organizations represented by the CAC might better serve and support HIV/AIDS-affected mothers and their families. We then came up with a plan. A team of researchers was assembled, and a formal research proposal was developed by AIDS Saskatoon staff, PWAS, and university-based social scientists. Funding was secured, a schedule for meetings with the CAC was set, approval from all representative Research Ethics Boards was sought and received, and a research office at AIDS Saskatoon was established. Consultation with the PWAS continued along the way. Over a year after our first meeting, Dennis and I were hanging recruitment posters in the drop-in centre. "We're finally off to the races," he declared.

This opening chapter sets the broader context for the project. Experiences with HIV/AIDS, like experiences with anything, do not unfold in neutral spaces. They take place in sites forged by a history of colonialism, disruption to Indigenous lifeways, European settlement, and cultural resilience. Experiences with HIV/AIDS are entangled with experiences with hepatitis C, opioid addiction, and poverty.

HIV/AIDS IN SASKATCHEWAN

Saskatchewan is the central prairie province in Canada. Geographically, it is very large at almost 652,000 square kilometres (252,000 square miles). With a population of only one million, though, it is considered to be "mid-sized" (Waiser 2005). There are many things that distinguish Saskatchewan. It has more hours of sunshine than any other province. It is one of the most tornado-active regions of the country. It is the only Canadian province with no natural border. Despite its very cold winters, Saskatchewan holds the record for the hottest temperature ever documented in the country (Environment Canada 2011). Saskatchewan also has the highest rates of HIV/AIDS in Canada.

In 2009, Saskatchewan's HIV incidence rate of 19.7 per 100,000 population was almost triple that of the national rate (6.9/100,000;

Tomas et al. 2015, 295). Between 2000 and 2009, the provincial rate rose by 488 per cent, with the sharpest increase occurring among women aged twenty to twenty-nine years (Saskatchewan Ministry of Health 2010). The epidemic in Saskatchewan has hit Indigenous communities particularly hard. Indigenous people represent 70 per cent of all newly diagnosed cases among men and 90 per cent among women (Saskatchewan Ministry of Health 2010, 4). Given that Indigenous people constitute 16 per cent of the provincial population, this is particularly striking. According to Health Canada, HIV rates across the province's 782 Indigenous reserves, settlements, and villages were eleven times higher than the national rate (representing a higher incidence than that of Rwanda and Nigeria; Vogel 2015, 793). HIV/AIDS-related death rates are four times the national average, with Indigenous people dying at over twice the rate of their non-Indigenous counterparts (Salloum 2015).

There has been ongoing news media interest in Saskatchewan's HIV/AIDS profile for almost a decade. Ken MacQueen's (2015) feature in Canada's leading news magazine, *Maclean's*, for example, declares that "Third World levels of HIV infection rates in one of the world's wealthiest countries are a national disgrace." Geoff Leo (2015) of the Canadian Broadcasting Company (CBC) decries the "Canadian crisis of African HIV rates" on the prairies, singling out Saskatchewan. Public health officers across the province have repeatedly and publicly expressed concern over the high HIV rates among Indigenous Peoples. In the words of the Elder who works with AIDS Saskatoon staff, it is "the plague of our times." The disproportionate rates of HIV/AIDS among Indigenous Peoples in Canada have their roots in the country's colonial history and state-sanctioned displacement, violence, and genocide. This is a history that unfolds on traditionally Indigenous lands and that targets the Indigenous Peoples of those lands.

Thomas King, recipient of the National Aboriginal Achievement Award and the Order of Canada, notes that "terminology is always a rascal" (2013, xiii). In this book, I generally use the term *Indigenous Peoples* to refer to "First Nations, Inuit, and Métis Peoples in Canada collectively" (Younging 2018, chap. 6). There are times, however, when I use other terms – *Indian, Native,* and *Aboriginal* – as they are used by the research participants or in the cited literature. The term *Indian* is a colonial misnomer, having its genesis in European expansion and missionary history. It is a derogatory and inappropriate term.

Yet it is used by some Indigenous people today as a way to draw attention to ongoing colonial structures. The term *Native* was "one of the most common descriptors of Indigenous Peoples in Canada, and other parts of the world, throughout the colonial period and into the 1980s" (Younging 2018, chap. 6). While it is not seen as derogatory as *Indian*, it is problematic "because of possible confusion with its wider definition of a 'local inhabitant or life form'" (chap. 6). The term *Aboriginal* is widely considered to be appropriate, but it is being replaced by the language in the 2007 United Nations *Declaration of Rights of Indigenous Peoples.*

For further clarification: Inuit are the Indigenous Peoples of the Arctic regions. *First Nations* is a term that came into common use in the 1980s to refer to Indigenous Peoples of the territories south of the Arctic Circle. These are the "separate nations that occupied territory before the arrival of the Europeans" (Younging 2018, chap. 6). There are 634 First Nations in Canada, representing fifty different languages. Seventy First Nations are located in Saskatchewan. Each Nation constitutes a governing body, but many unite to form a tribal council. In Saskatchewan, sixty-one First Nations are affiliated with one of nine tribal councils that provide shared and centralized services. The Saskatoon Tribal Council, for example, represents seven First Nations and provides community justice programs, housing services, education leadership, and child and family services (among other programs).

Métis Peoples are of mixed Indigenous and European (predominantly French) heritage. The Métis National Council (MNC) defines Métis as those who self-identify as such, are distinct from other Indigenous Peoples, are descendants of the historic Métis Nation in southern Manitoba, and who are accepted by that Nation (Gaudry 2009). According to the MNC, the Métis share an ancestral language (Michif) and a traditional homeland in British Columbia, Alberta, Saskatchewan, Manitoba, Ontario, the Northwest Territories, and the northern United States. This definition has been challenged, and claims to a broader Métis homeland have been made by the Congress of Aboriginal Peoples, among others (Posluns 2007). However, the participants in this research all fall within the MNC definition, locating their heritage in Prairie Canada.

The rights of First Nations, Métis, and Inuit Peoples have been historically tied to state-imposed definitions of their identity. The 1867

Constitution Act gave the federal government (rather than the provincial governments) responsibility for "the Indians and the Land reserved for the Indians." Two court cases (the first in 1939 and the second in 2013) established that all Indigenous Peoples in Canada are included in this reference to "Indians" (Vasiliki 2013, 84–5). It is the Indian Act of 1876 that imposed restrictive definitions on who could be designated as a "status Indian," creating a distinction between those who have federal recognition and those who do not. As Thomas King explains, the Indian Act itself "does more than just define Legal Indians. It has been the main mechanism for controlling the lives and destinies of Legal Indians in Canada, and throughout the life of the Act, amendments have been made to the original documents to fine-tune this control." He continues:

> An 1881 amendment prohibited the sale of agricultural produce by Legal Indians in the prairie provinces, to keep them from competing with White farmers. An 1885 amendment prohibited religious ceremonies and dances. A 1905 amendment allowed the removal of Aboriginal people from reserves that were too close to White towns of more than 8,000 residents. A 1911 amendment allowed municipalities and companies to expropriate portions of reserves, without the permission of the band, for roads, railways, and other public works. A 1914 amendment required Legal Indians to get official permission before appearing in Aboriginal costume in any dance, show, exhibition, stampede, or pageant.... A 1930 amendment banned Legal Indians from playing pool if they did it too often and wasted their time to the detriment of themselves and their families. (King 2013, 70–1)

The Constitution Act and the Indian Act were (and still are) instruments of assimilation and control. Duncan Campbell Scott, head of Canada's Department of Indian Affairs from 1913 to 1932, is quoted as saying, "I want to get rid of the Indian problem. Our objective is to continue until there is not a single Indian in Canada that has not been absorbed into the body politic and there is no Indian question, and no Indian Department" (King 2013, 72).

Predating the Constitution Act and the Indian Act were two key pieces of legislation – the 1842 Bagot Commission Report and the 1857

Gradual Civilisation Act – that established a residential school system (Miller 1996). The purpose of the schools was to separate Indigenous children from their home communities, assimilating them into European settler societies. Between 1840 and 1996, some 150,000 Indigenous children were taken from their home communities and placed in these schools. James Waldram (2004, 229–30) explains that residential schools were "total institutions" in which "every aspect of the child's life was regulated. Sleeping, eating, playing, working, and learning were all regulated [and] supported by strict codes of conduct and corporal punishment." Residential school staff imposed uncompromising rules prohibiting children from speaking their own languages, requiring them to wear European-style clothing, and demanding adherence to Christianity.

Canada's Truth and Reconciliation Commission (2015a, 2015b) documents thousands of testimonies of former students who were traumatized by physical and sexual violence, starvation, psychological distress, and emotional abuse while attending these schools. The Aboriginal Healing Foundation (1999, 5) draws on hundreds of studies across the medical and social sciences to assert that the intergenerational effects of residential school trauma have eroded family cohesion and Indigenous health: "When there is no support for dealing with it, trauma will be passed from one generation to the next. Higher rates of addiction, abuse, and child neglect can be found in families of residential school survivors" (Olynick et al. 2016). Children in these homes often grow to be adults who have learned coping skills (including addictive and avoidant behaviours) that are deleterious to their health.

The apprehension of children and the disruption to Indigenous families did not end when the majority of residential schools closed. Beginning in the early 1960s, provincial and federal welfare systems apprehended Indigenous children who were believed to be in harm's way and placed them in Euro-Canadian foster and adoptive homes. As I have argued elsewhere, "It is important to note that in some cases children were removed from homes because they were facing undue hardships, and the charges of wrongdoing were substantiated by Aboriginal and non-Aboriginal authorities alike.... However, in most other cases, the charges of parental abuse and neglect were flimsy at best and reflected long-standing racist biases towards Aboriginal communities and their residents" (Downe 2014, 23).

Once in a system of rotating foster and state care, many children lost contact with their families and home communities. The apprehension of children in what is now known as the "sixties scoop" was driven by the same colonial agenda as the residential school system: to disrupt and diminish Indigenous communities. Maureen McEvoy and Judith Daniluk (1995, 223) conclude that the apprehension rate in the 1960s was "so high that some reserves lost nearly a generation of children to child welfare authorities." Award-winning Métis author Maria Campbell has spoken about the fear and distrust aroused by the decades of child apprehension and the intransigence of government officials who arrived unannounced in communities to take the children. This was, she stated, "the time of the black car" (in Anderson 2000, 162). By the late 1980s, the apprehension of Indigenous children had slowed, but the overall rate was still six times higher than the national average (Hanvey and Avard 1994). It has remained high ever since. Throughout the AIDS Saskatoon research, both Indigenous and non-Indigenous participants often described the history of child apprehension as having lasting individual and collective effects.

Child apprehensions occurred alongside other damaging colonial policies: the stripping of "Indian status" from women who married non-Indigenous men, the forced removal of entire communities from their lands, and disenfranchisement from political office (among others). From the 1950s onwards, thousands of Indigenous women in Canada and the United States have been forcibly or unknowingly sterilized so that they could not have (any more) children. Karen Stote (2012) and Leonardo Pegoraro (2015) explain that, like coercive measures in the past, this was done to destabilize Indigenous populations, communities, and families.

Throughout the 1980s and 1990s, Indigenous communities were under a different siege. Women, men, and children were disappearing from their homes. Lists of missing Indigenous persons were growing each year as the number of kidnappings, sexual assaults, and murders increased (Downe 2014). According to the final report of the National Inquiry into Missing and Murdered Indigenous Women and Girls (2019), Indigenous women face a much higher risk of kidnapping, murder, and sexual assault than non-Indigenous women. "There are a lot of us here who have loved ones who are gone. Sisters, mothers, grandmothers, just vanished," Dennis said. "I don't know anybody who doesn't live with fear."

SYNDEMIC CONNECTIONS

Years of state-sanctioned genocide, violence, and discrimination against Indigenous Peoples have taken their toll. They have culminated in what Paul Farmer (2004) calls structural violence: the chronic and systemic disadvantages faced by those who live in impoverished and oppressive contexts. The HIV/AIDS epidemic that now ravages Indigenous populations of the Canadian prairies is a product of this violence. This epidemic, however, is not a stand-alone health issue. Across Canada, it is linked with hepatitis C virus (HCV), a blood-borne virus that infects the liver. Both HIV and HCV are transmitted through shared syringes and injection drug use. Self-medication with drugs of all kinds, including opiates and opioids, is an avoidant coping strategy often employed among those who live with the effects of trauma, unrelenting fear, pain, ill health, social ostracism, and poverty.

Syndemic theory, introduced by medical anthropologist Merrill Singer (2009), provides a framework for identifying and analyzing overlapping health and social conditions. Whereas biomedical models of comorbidity position each co-occurring condition as distinct from but additive to the others, syndemic models position the conditions as synergistically interrelated (Singer et al. 2011). The interaction among the conditions results in the overall burden of illness and harm that is more than the sum of its parts. Syndemic conditions are multiplicative rather than additive.

The first syndemic identified by Singer in the mid-1990s was SAVA (Substance Abuse-Violence-AIDS). "From the syndemic perspective AIDS, drug use, and violence in particular social contexts are so entwined with each other and each is so significantly shaped by the presence of the other two that if one tries to understand them as distinct things in the world, it is hard to conceive of them accurately" (Singer 2009, 31). Throughout the AIDS Saskatoon research, the synergistic connections among HIV, HCV, addiction, and injection drug use were driven by poverty, intergenerational trauma, and the legacy of colonialism. Together, they constitute the Saskatchewan HIV syndemic.

All components of the HIV syndemic are significant in the lives of the thirty women and twenty-three men who regularly access the services of AIDS Saskatoon and who participated in this research. The connections among HIV, HCV, and injection drug use are particularly significant. Whereas injection drug use accounts for 13 per cent of all new HIV cases at the national level, it is responsible for over 77 per cent of new cases in Saskatchewan (PHAC 2015, 10). Canada's "opioid crisis" has hit Saskatchewan particularly hard (Special Advisory Committee 2019). Opioids are synthetic pain-relieving drugs (such as fentanyl, heroin, oxycodone, and hydromorphene) that can result in a high or sensation of euphoria. The effects are particularly intense when the drug is injected intravenously. An opioid use disorder – an addiction – develops when an individual is psychologically and/or physiologically dependent on the drug and keeps using it despite its harmful effects.

The history of how addiction has been understood medically, politically, and culturally is diverse, long, and fascinating. Ancient texts from India, China, Egypt, Greece, and the Americas are filled with references to psychoactive drugs, usually in affiliation with religion. With the rise of Western medicine, herbalists and apothecaries identified the curative, analgesic, and preventive properties of plant-derived drugs, and state authorities implemented regulatory policies. Marc-Antoine Crocq (2007, 356) explains that as early as the seventeenth century in Britain, the compulsive use of drugs was well known and was a matter of great debate. Was it a disease or a sin, a medical or moral matter? The pendulum of popular and professional opinion on this debate continues to swing. Most medical researchers now agree that substance use disorders are diseases – injuries to the brain, in fact – that make treatment of addiction much more complicated than just saying "no to drugs."

As part of the broader HIV/AIDS syndemic, addiction is also grounded in, and influenced by, local social environments. Paul Gahlinger (2001, 201) argues that people use drugs illegally (that is, without medical supervision and in violation of regulatory policies) primarily to numb themselves: "The opiates, barbiturates, methaqualone, and other drugs have historically been taken to help the user escape pain, dissociate from the body, and achieve a sort of mental vacation." The PWAS at AIDS Saskatoon explain their drug use in these terms. They describe needing a break from the pain, wanting a respite from illness, "a way to get away from all the hate" (as Dennis once put it). They are not alone.

Angela Garcia (2010) identifies the social roots of addiction in her research with Hispanic residents of the Española Valley in New Mexico. She argues that the widespread heroin addiction in the region is inseparable from the local history from which many Spanish-speaking residents, particularly those living in poverty, want to escape. Northern New Mexico has been a "site of colonial exploitation and transformation for more than four centuries. Today, locals passionately express the material and cultural losses that resulted from the region's embattled past – in particular, the loss of Spanish and Mexican land grants – and they ... understand its heroin problem as a contemporary consequence" (Garcia 2010, 10). Aspects of drug use that are commonly represented as highly individual, including getting high and overdosing, are informed by and best understood in relation to the historical and social contexts of dispossession.

The forty-six participants in the AIDS Saskatoon research who identify as Indigenous – Cree, Dene, or Métis – expressed a similar dispossession. They seek a reprieve from the colonial history that constrains their lives in social and material ways. For the seven participants who identify as White, the historical and colonial context is also important. "I am a White guy walking with my Aboriginal brothers," Ben responded when I asked him to describe himself. "I don't got to live with the crap that the Aboriginal guys do, but we get painted with the same brush so I get a small taste of what they have to put up with every day. I don't know how any of us would live through it without AIDS Saskatoon."

COMMUNITY-ENGAGED RESEARCH METHODOLOGIES

AIDS Saskatoon is located on the Treaty Six territory in Saskatchewan. The agency serves the cities of Saskatoon (population 270,000) and Prince Albert (population 35,000), as well as the smaller northern and central communities encompassed by Treaties Five, Eight, and Ten. The majority of PWAS at AIDS Saskatoon currently reside in Saskatoon itself. As the largest city in the province, Saskatoon is a draw for those from smaller areas who are looking for city-based work and services. The city is home to the University of Saskatchewan, three hospitals, the Saskatoon Tribal Council, Métis Nation of Saskatchewan, the Central Urban Métis Federation, and is the headquarters for the province's large mining companies. There are three potash mines and one salt mine within commuting distance of Saskatoon, and many of the men who participated in this research have worked, at one time or another, in these mines.

With a median personal income of $40,642, Saskatoon holds the middle rank among Canada's major metropolitan areas in regard to income earned by those over fifteen (Statistics Canada 2017a). However, income is not equitably distributed throughout the city. Evelyn Peters and Tyler McCreary (2008) explain that there is a concentration of low-income residents on the city's west side, which is separated from the more affluent east side by the South Saskatchewan River. Moreover, those who live in poverty – meaning those who do not have the financial and productive resources to ensure sustainable livelihoods and meet basic needs (United Nations 2018) – are further concentrated into three core west-side neighbourhoods adjacent to the downtown business district. These neighbourhoods lack basic services such as grocery stores and schools, and rental housing is often in ill repair. They are home to the majority of the city's Indigenous residents (Fawcett, Walker, and Greene 2015; Peters and McCreary 2008). At over 10 per cent of the city's total citizenry, Saskatoon's urban Indigenous population is one of the largest in Canada, second only to Winnipeg. There is, therefore, a clear and racialized divide between the affluent neighbourhoods on the east side and the core neighbourhoods on the west side.

Saskatoon is routinely among the top five cities in Canada's Crime Severity Index, which calculates the rates and severity of police-reported crimes. Although violent crime was down in the city by 2 per cent in 2018, drug-related crime had increased significantly. According to a CBC (2019) report, there were 249 methamphetamine-related incidents reported to police that year, a 500 per cent increase from 2014. Police services suspect the rise in methamphetamine use "is contributing to an uptick in other types of crime, including property and violent crimes," the majority of which occur on the west side (CBC 2019).

AIDS Saskatoon is located in one of the west side's core neighbourhoods. It serves many of the people rendered vulnerable by the systemic racism, violence, and crime in the city. The agency opened in 1986 with only two staff members who offered support services to those most affected by the epidemic at the time: gay White men. Peer- and counsellor-support programs provided a refuge from the homophobia and judgment that dominated public responses to the newly identified HIV/AIDS epidemic. The United Nations Global Program (now UNAIDS) declared the first World AIDS Day on December 1, 1988. It was also on this date that the archived notes of AIDS Saskatoon staff made the first reference to Indigenous men among the PWAS. "We need to make sure that we are culturally appropriate in our work," the staff member wrote in capital letters (Downe et al. 2016, 4). From that time onward, a clear commitment to meeting the needs of Indigenous as well as non-Indigenous PWAS fuelled AIDS Saskatoon's work.

Since its inception, AIDS Saskatoon has adhered to principles of harm reduction. This is a PWAS-centred and justice-oriented approach to reducing the harms associated with the HIV/AIDS syndemic. It rejects the punitive and coercive approaches to addiction and drug use adopted in criminal justice and health care systems. As the outreach coordinator explained it, "We're all about supporting the PWAS on their journey to be as healthy as they can be. We meet them where they're at, and let them lead the way." Reducing harm associated with drug use, HIV, HCV, and all the other challenges in the PWAS' lives is a process that unfolds as frequently in the drop-in centre – which came to be known as "The 601" (shorthand for the address: 601 33rd Street West) – as it does in staff offices.

This ethnography is rooted in AIDS Saskatoon and The 601. It tells the story of the primarily Indigenous Peoples who access these services in order to care for themselves and their families. This is a local story but one about people whose experiences with HIV/AIDS have similarities and connections to those around the globe. It is a story that is largely untold but not unique. Poverty and racism are structures and forces faced by millions in HIV-affected communities throughout sub-Saharan Africa (Iliffe 2006). In his historical ethnography, John Iliffe (2006, 112) argues that the HIV/AIDS epidemic in Africa was not one epidemic but four: "first the virus, then disease, next death, and finally societal decomposition, each superimposed upon its predecessors." In Saskatchewan, the forced disruption and dislocation of Indigenous societies underpins the HIV virus, disease, and death. The stories of suffering that emerged through this AIDS Saskatoon research echo those told by Iliffe, but the linear progression that Iliffe traces toward societal decomposition is a very different one in this case. Societal decomposition is not the end stage for those living with HIV/AIDS in Saskatchewan. It is a daily threat and historical reality. Philip Setel's (1999, 237) work on HIV/AIDS in Kilimanjaro in northern Tanzania similarly demonstrates that HIV/AIDS is bound up with "disordered relations of power from the interpersonal to the international." This applies to the HIV/AIDS syndemic in Saskatchewan where histories of colonialism, child apprehension, poverty, and violence have left indelible marks on individual, as well as collective, bodies. What distinguishes this book from Iliffe's and Setel's, and other such books, is the focus on HIV/AIDS and family experience as it is mediated in and around one particular place, AIDS Saskatoon. It is the attention to daily and local experiences that allows us to see what it means to live a life and to care for family amidst a pandemic that is shaped by structural forces reaching from the global sphere to the small house that serves as AIDS Saskatoon's home.

Over the course of this research, my research assistants and I spent approximately eighty hours in The 601, getting to know PWAS, visiting, and helping with regular tasks (making coffee, updating computers, folding donated clothes). This kind of participant observation is the bedrock of ethnography, an immersive approach to exploring the cultural dynamics of a community. We learned that "soul food" meant the nutritious hot lunches that were provided monthly (and then weekly). We learned that kin terms such as *mother* and *father* refer not only to biological parents but to anyone who assumes a primary caregiving role to children. *Family* means an emotionally close network of people who have affection for, responsibilities to, and expectations of each other. The interspersion of Cree words throughout everyday conversations and interviews is not only a stylistic expression, it is a political act, a claiming of place and heritage. Stories about family are a way to communicate the importance of kinship more broadly. We learned that use of the term *client* to refer to people who accessed services is abhorred by AIDS Saskatoon staff because of its corporate connotations. "PWAS" (people who access services) is the preferred term. We learned how to laugh at good-natured teasing and to respond without judgment when the PWAS relapsed in their journey toward health.

Ethnography also involves talking to people one on one. We began with open-ended, narrative-style interviews, allowing the PWAS to set the direction of our conversations. Forty participants, twenty-four women and sixteen men, sat down with me on two separate occasions. In all but three of these eighty interviews, family, parenting, and children figured centrally. At times, the one-to-one interviews were interrupted by other participants who wanted to join the conversation, shifting the encounter from an individual interview to a small and spontaneous focus group. This is the nature of ethnographic interviewing. It is driven more by the participants than the researcher, revealing more about community dynamics, interpersonal relationships, and overall interest in the research topic than other methodologies would ever reveal.

A photovoice project constituted the second component of the study. This is now a common methodology in the social and health sciences. Participants take photographs of what they feel is relevant in their lives and then discuss the images. It is a "community-based action research method that is intended to empower those who have traditionally been ... subject to harmful representations" (Shankar 2016, 158). The images produced through photovoice are both descriptive and transformative. Photovoice allows research participants to refocus their attention on everyday and often taken-for-granted relationships, landmarks, and fixtures, giving them rejuvenated meaning. There can be broader political implications as well. Jennifer Poudrier and Roanne Thomas-Maclean (2009, 308–9) point out that "where pictures may be worth a thousand words, images captured by marginalized persons explained through a story can have potential for sociocultural and policy change."

In the AIDS Saskatoon research, disposable analogue cameras were given to thirteen participants who were asked to take pictures of the people, places, and things that best reflect what it means to be a parent in the context of HIV/AIDS in Saskatchewan. Over 230 photographs were taken, and follow-up interviews were conducted with each participant. The interviews centred on that which Marcus Banks (2001, 7)

Photo 1. Francine's seeded dandelion

identifies as fundamental to the visual analyses: the content of the image, why it was taken, and the meaning that the participant assigns to the image.

Francine, a Cree mother of four adult children, took a close-up photograph of a seeded dandelion (Photo 1). "I love this picture," she explained, holding it to her heart. "I like to blow on the seeds and make wishes. I want all my kids to be ok. People here in the city mow the dandelions down and they don't realize how important wishing can be. This picture reminds me of all the wishes that have come true ... and all of them that haven't. We need a wish program here in The 601. Let's help get these seeds in the ground."

This one image provided a way for Francine to reflect on the future she desires for her children and for a program that might allow the wishes of the PWAS at AIDS Saskatoon to come true. There is, I learned, a hopefulness among the PWAS that is unshakeable.

Throughout the narrative and photovoice interviews, research participants spoke frequently about the health care and social services that they regularly access. In order to explore this more systematically, I conducted forty-eight program access interviews with twenty-seven women and twenty-one men. These interviews focused on the benefits, access points, barriers, and drawbacks of the specific services that research participants use, need, and seek. We learned that twenty-two of the participants were regularly accessing the medical methadone program for addiction, that all of the participants regularly sought assistance from AIDS Saskatoon staff, and that they never initiated contact with police or Child and Family Services (CFS).

Forty participants were prescribed anti-retroviral therapeutics (ART) to manage their HIV. Of those, twenty-seven routinely sought medical care for the resulting side effects, including nausea, light-headedness, and lipodystrophy (the loss of subcutaneous fat in some areas and an accumulation in other areas, creating an unevenness in skin appearance). The secondary medications that the participants need to manage the side effects of ART are usually unaffordable and are rarely covered by provincial health plans. Eight interviews were also conducted with AIDS Saskatoon staff, focused on how the agency itself was identifying and responding to the needs and strengths of mothers and families.

All ethnographic interviews are shaped as much by the researcher as by the participants. The rapport we establish, the attributes we share, and the tones we set affect what participants tell us and how our work might be of benefit to them. *Reflexivity* is the term that is often used to describe a critical reflection on our researcher role. Although the term itself is somewhat contested, if we take it to mean the "grappling with self-awareness and politics, and how we frame reality, as we conduct our research and as we write" (Mayan 2009, 138), then it is important to any research that grounds itself in participants' world views and daily realities. I came to AIDS Saskatoon with ten years of experience conducting collaborative research with Indigenous Peoples in Saskatchewan, as well as a lifetime of respect for First Nations, Métis, and Inuit sovereignty. Still, as a non-Indigenous anthropologist with a safe home, relatively good health, and a steady income, my position in relation to the participants was one of difference. I was prepared to talk with participants (and anyone who asked) about my commitment to Indigenous rights, as well as my familial connections to Indigenous communities. I am a mother to two women of Cree heritage, and my paternal grandmother (Anne Downe) was honoured by the Tsuu T'ina Nation with a ceremonial name (as were all her grandchildren, including me). An exhibit in recognition of Anne's work in support of Indigenous self-determination (especially in education) was displayed in the Tsuu T'ina museum for ten years. However, perhaps because they work with non-Indigenous service providers every day, the participants were not particularly interested in any of this. They were much more interested in talking about what this project might potentially offer to them as mothers and fathers who face insurmountable odds of ill health and stigma. The participants wanted to know how their stories would be represented in publications and presentations, the extent to which verbatim transcription would be used, and how Cree words would be incorporated.

The demographic and socio-economic differences between the research participants and me never went away, but they were folded into our lively, respectful, and ultimately trusting relationships. I became a grandmother (four times over) during the course of this research. The participants helped me celebrate my new status. Several of the women with whom I became particularly close referred to me as *kohkum* (the Cree word for "grandmother") and then, in a nod to my Irish background, helped me choose "Nana" as my grandmotherly moniker. It also happened that my mother died as I was writing this book. Grief temporarily stole the sense of familiarity and groundedness that having my mother in the world gave me. I lost my bearings. But this experience also connected me anew to the stories of the research participants. When I replayed the recordings of our interviews to double-check the accuracy of my transcription and analysis, I heard the exhaustion in the women's voices and a thick sadness in their stories. Unlike mine, however, the research participants' grief was (and remains) rooted in a broader context of long-standing oppression, displacement, and fear. The majority of the mothers with whom I worked on this project have had their bearings repeatedly ripped from them. They live amidst the historical and looming loss associated with family separation, cultural uprootedness, forced community relocation, injury, insecurity, assault, and death. After I lost my mother, the enormity and chronicity of the research participants' grief became so much clearer, not only because of the renewed emotional connection but also because of the structural contrasts between my life and theirs. If I was struggling amidst grief to recover my personal bearings, what struggle is undertaken by those who are denied the resources and privileges that I have at my daily disposal? How can researchers represent the struggle of those who seek not only to recover their personal bearings but also to rebuild and strengthen their community of support?

Anthropologists venture to address questions such as these through systematic inquiry, ethnographic engagement, and critical reflexivity. We must be aware of how our own cultural histories, privileges, challenges, and demographics position us in relation to the community members with whom we partner. We must be vigilant, however, to ensure that our personal reflections do not eclipse the lives of the participants who entrust us to represent the aggregate stories that *their* narratives tell.

CONCLUSION: DECOLONIZING RESEARCH

In all, 152 interviews, constituting almost 320 hours, were recorded. Some 500 inductive codes emerged from the 4,700 pages of interview transcripts and 61 pages of participant observation notes, culminating in the analysis presented in the coming chapters. The story that opened here continues in Chapter 2 with a more detailed discussion of the participants, their families, and the importance of kin-centred approaches to the anthropological study of HIV/AIDS. Chapters 3 and 4 describe what motherhood, fatherhood, and parental care in the local context of HIV/AIDS entail. The Cree term *kikosewin* captures the broader family dynamics that sustain health and provide comfort in times of suffering and death. Chapter 5 explores how loss marks the lives of HIV-affected mothers. The analysis centres on participants' conceptualization of *mescinewin*, the loss of an entire family to disease. Chapter 6 contrasts the devastation of loss with stories of familial love and home. The sense of hopefulness that Francine captured so beautifully in her description of a seeded dandelion endures.

The reliance on the participants' words and stories to frame the overall analysis is informed by efforts to decolonize research. Over twenty years ago, Maori scholar Linda Tuhiwai Smith (1999) wrote passionately about the history of exploitation of Indigenous Peoples by researchers from all fields, including anthropology. Indigenous "beliefs" were assessed (often negatively) in relation to European "knowledge," the unequal footing of each already established at the outset of the research. This inequality is redressed, Smith argues, by reframing our analyses in ways that honour and embolden Indigenous concepts. Jennifer Poudrier and Roanne Thomas-Maclean (2009, 309) similarly advocate a centring of Indigenous knowledge, experiences, and values so that they are not assessed by European standards of correctness but are represented in their own right. Working with the CAC and attending to the details of what participants shared with me, I doubled back time and time again to each participant, asking for clarification, making sure I was getting it right. "You know my words better than I do now," Dennis laughed, playfully calling me "Boomerang" because I would always come back.

2

Family

> While many important studies have highlighted the biomedical realities of HIV as they intersect with cultural, social, and structural factors, I take as my main premise that AIDS is fundamentally a kinship disease.
>
> – *Ellen Block and Will McGrath (2019, 6–7)*

Lisa was the first participant in the research. She approached me only a few minutes after Dennis and I had put up recruitment posters in The 601. Her two children, an eight-year-old son and a five-year-old daughter, had been removed from her care earlier that week after Lisa was charged with her third drug-related offence. Lisa's drug offences are usually minor, but they signal to Saskatoon Tribal Council's Child and Family Services (CFS) that she may be having difficulty handling the pressures of motherhood amidst treatments for HIV and HCV. "I started using [drugs] again after months of being clean," Lisa said in a whisper. "I got the world on my shoulders right now. I'm so sick all the time. Everything hurts. I wanted to feel good again. Just for a night." Lisa had visible bruises on her face and the side of her neck. She never explained how she got them but she repeatedly winced with pain.

Lisa was quiet and shy at first. Originally from a northern Dene community, she was placed in a Saskatoon foster home when she was nine years old. She lived in a total of six foster homes over the next eight years. At seventeen, she moved in with her boyfriend. Her son was born the following year and her daughter three years after that. "I had things together pretty good," Lisa recalled. "But then [my boyfriend] and me broke up, and I had no place to go, and I got scared. I dropped the kids at my aunt's place 'cause I knew they'd be safe there. I hit the streets." The following eight months were a blur. Lisa moved from one friend's place to another. She was often homeless in between. She sold sex to survive. Her addiction to hydrocodone, morphine, and fentanyl grew stronger. She cannot remember how often she shared needles with friends and strangers, "but it was at least a dozen times, probably more." On a cold spring night, a passerby called an ambulance after finding Lisa unconscious in a public park. At the hospital, Lisa consented to blood tests and was diagnosed as HIV- and HCV-positive. "It was a wakeup call," she declared. "I was scared straight."

One year later (to the very day that marked her breakup with her former boyfriend), Lisa had a job in a commercial laundromat. She moved into the apartment next door to her aunt. "Everything was finally going good again," Lisa recalled. "I learned that nobody can do nothing on their own. You got to have family." She continued, "I *really* like the kids' foster mom. I mean, I *really* like her. She loves the kids and takes good care of them, and she knows that I take care of them when I can. It's like me and her are on the Mom Team. And [my] auntie is in there, too. And my 601 family here. The kids got lots of love around them. So do I. That's what makes me a good mom even when I don't got the kids with me." Lisa's voice became louder and more animated as she described her "mom team," saying, "I'm a good mom 'cause I got a good team, simple as that."

Mothering in the context of HIV/AIDS, however, is anything but simple. Nausea from the ART treatments, body temperature fluctuations from methadone treatments, general fatigue and irritability, housing insecurities, and harsh public criticism take a cumulative toll on women's health and their abilities to live up to high ideals of parental care. Relying on others for help and support is essential for overwhelmed, poor, and ill mothers. "There's not nobody who could do it on their own," Lisa explained. "Good moms got good teams, but we don't get points for being part of the team. We just get crap that we can't do it all ourselves."

In this first interview, Lisa summarized what ultimately came to be the central theme of the research. Collective care is a necessary form of mothering for women living with or otherwise affected by HIV/AIDS. More than that, collective care represents an ethos of social interconnectedness. It provides a sense of belonging and safety. It is a cultural touchstone in many Indigenous communities not only in Canada but across the world. A survey of the Human Relations Area Files (the largest database of cross-cultural resources in the world) reveals that collective responsibility for family well-being is more common than individualistic models of care. All of the AIDS Saskatoon mothers and fathers with whom I spoke shared a similar commitment to collective care. "It's not like we're all the same," Lisa explained. "But we're not all that different neither. And when it comes to looking after our kids, we all know that we're in it together. We don't know no other way."

The participants' ways of knowing are the culmination of their personal as well as collective histories, their individual choices, and the structural forces that have shaped those choices. This chapter introduces the participants and the social and historical contexts in which they are situated. I also locate this project more directly in the anthropological literature that is most relevant, and to which this research and an understanding of the "mom teams" may contribute.

RESEARCH PARTICIPANTS AND THEIR FAMILIES

Twenty-four of the thirty women who participated in this research had biological children. The other six identified as mothers through their caregiving responsibilities to and affection for children in their families. At no point did a hierarchy between biological or non-biological mothers emerge, although non-biological mothers often felt particularly vulnerable to CFS scrutiny and intervention. All of the women with whom I spoke agreed that a mother is a woman who mothers. A family is a kin group that collectively cares for children and elders.

Families are sites of strength and struggle. The struggles faced by the research participants are not only health related. They are also economic, intensely so for the forty-six Indigenous participants. In Canada, Indigenous men and women are twice as likely as non-Indigenous men and women to live below the low-income threshold (O'Donnell and

Wallace 2015). Indigenous students leave school at a greater rate than their non-Indigenous counterparts. With limited education, safe and secure employment is hard to find. Without steady employment, financial insecurity continues and the income inequalities between Indigenous and non-Indigenous people grow (Kolahdooz et al. 2015). Economic inequities coupled with political and cultural marginalization take a serious toll on Indigenous women's health in particular. Paula Arriaga (2016) reports that Indigenous women across Canada have higher rates of chronic disorders such as arthritis, asthma, high blood pressure, and anxiety disorders than do non-Indigenous women. First Nations and Métis women in Saskatchewan are less likely than non-Indigenous women to have a regular doctor, and almost 20 per cent of Indigenous women therefore have unmet health needs (compared to 13 per cent of non-Indigenous women). Bearing the stress of chronic illness and income inequality diminishes women's overall well-being, as well as their abilities to pursue opportunities for employment and education (Arriaga 2016). "I would really love to be heading off to school, learning how to do things," Lisa noted, "but I feel so sick so much. And I just can't afford it."

Lisa is among the twenty-three women with whom I worked on this project who did not complete high school. She is also among the twenty-seven women who had insufficient financial resources for basic necessities: "I try to work a couple of jobs to make rent, but I got to look after the kids. And buy their clothes and bus passes and school supplies and meds. Then I got nothing left over for food." Lynda, a thirty-four-year-old Cree mother, explained that the stuttered speech she had as a child returns whenever she experiences high degrees of anxiety associated with financial stress, discrimination, and ill health. Self-medication with illicit opioids is one of the few things that provide relief from the unrelenting anxiety. "It's th-the only th-thing th-that makes th-the p-p-pressure st-st-stop," she said through tears of frustration. It was through her drug-related use of needles that Lynda – like Lisa, Janice, and nineteen other research participants – became infected with HIV and HCV. The remaining eleven women did not disclose their HIV or HCV status to me but they openly acknowledged that they are aware of their ongoing risk for the infection.

All of the research participants have a history of opioid addiction. Sixteen of the mothers with whom I spoke used opioid drugs regularly at the time of this research. The remaining fourteen women had been sober for at least six consecutive months but acknowledged a history of injection drug use and addiction. As a result, most of the women participating in this research had undergone home assessments by Social Services to ensure that their children were safe. Twelve women had had at least one (and usually all) of their underage children temporarily or permanently removed from their care within the previous two years. Another thirteen women, including those who had undergone home assessments by the Saskatchewan Ministry of Social Services or the First Nations CFS, lived with the fear that their children would be apprehended. "When Raylynne's youngest daughter was born, [CFS] just snatched the baby away right in the hospital," Lisa explained, recalling her friend's experience. "Raylynne got the baby back but she had to get a lawyer and fight real hard. All of us Aboriginal moms, all of us HIV moms, we live with this nightmare all the time."

Of the twelve AIDS Saskatoon mothers who had their children removed from their care, three (including Raylynne) had their babies taken away at birth. There is no provincial mandate to separate infants from HIV-positive mothers. There is, however, a mandate to remove infants from the care of mothers who use drugs. "They don't got to prove that we're using [drugs]," Lisa claimed. "They just got to suspect we're using [drugs] and they snatch the baby." Indeed, CFS relies on health care providers to issue birth alerts, signalling that an expectant mother requires assessment and surveillance. The grounds for these alerts are not always clear. They can entail suspicion of drug and/or alcohol use or more tangible signs of risk. It is also unclear how decisions are made about when a baby should be removed from a mother's care while the CFS assessment is underway. There is plenty of room for sound, professional judgment to inform the process. There is also plenty of room for stigma and racism to taint it. According to the women who participated in this research, the process is characterized more by the latter. A similar colonial logic that resulted in forced sterilizations of Indigenous women and over 150 years of residential schools may still be at play given that almost 90 per cent of children who are taken into state care in Saskatchewan and Manitoba are Indigenous (Edwards 2018).

As will be discussed in greater detail in Chapter 4, the research ultimately expanded to include fathers as well. The AIDS Saskatoon PWAS and the Community Advisory Committee felt strongly that involving fathers in the research would provide a more in-depth understanding of the dynamics of collective care that characterize their lives. Twenty-three men joined the thirty women as research participants. Like the women, the majority (twenty) of the men identified as Cree, Dene, or Métis. Neil was the only man who did not have biological children. However, he identified as a father because of his caregiving responsibilities to his six nieces and nephews. The men share the women's experiences with poverty, addiction and drug use, and HIV. All twenty-three men had used injection drugs on multiple occasions in the five years previous to the research. At the time of this project, eleven men used drugs regularly while the other twelve had been sober for at least six consecutive months.

All the participants knew each other in one way or another, most as friends and fellow PWAS. There were six sets of family members. One group of eight participants defined each other with kin terms: children, siblings, cousins, parents, aunts, uncles. Another group of three participants were sisters. And there were four couples who, regardless of legal marital status, identified each other as husband or wife. The research participants recognized these kin connections as critically important, but they also emphasized that The 601 itself had a family-like atmosphere. "We're a loud, big, messy family," Janice said with a laugh. Family, then, not only defines the specific relationships that some PWAS had with others but is a defining principle for AIDS Saskatoon's drop-in centre. As Lynda put it, "I can't count on much, but I can count on the people here having my back. They're like blood to me and my boy."

KINSHIP

Whether in relation to The 601 or another aspect of their lives, the research participants regularly emphasized the importance of family. "Don't matter if it's blood or not," Sally explained. "You love somebody like family, then you got a home with them. That's how we always did it on the rez." Johnny was particularly emotional in talking about the role that family plays in the life of his children: "We are just always there. There's not a day when we don't check on mom, when we don't check on each other. Our family is a knot. We're all tied up together."

Kinship is a tightly woven fabric. It holds a central place in all human societies and has drawn the attention of anthropologists since the inception of the discipline. Indeed, "there is little doubt that [kinship] has been treated as the single most important aspect of society, as far as anthropological theory is concerned" (Barnard 2002, 784). Anthropologists in the early twentieth century were primarily concerned with the general structure of kinship and its connection to political structures. They focused on how biological and cultural categories of relations were operationalized to maintain or challenge social systems and resource access. In the early years of the discipline, there was little interest in families as social units of intimacy and nurturance. Networks of economic and political power, not networks of care, drew most attention. These initial studies were also highly gendered. Attention was largely focused on men and their status-related activities within kin networks. Men's nurturing work and virtually all of women's work were overlooked.

Over the past forty years or so, there has been a significant shift in the study of kinship. It is now understood to be "*made* in houses through the intimate sharing of space, food, and nurturance that goes on within domestic space" (Carsten 2004, chap. 1). Kinship is understood as a site where cultural meaning is constructed and negotiated as well as a political and economic structure. The newly emerging "kinship studies" (as it is now known) brought women to the foreground of anthropological scholarship and fuelled the parallel rise of the anthropology of gender. Today, an intersectional approach to kinship attends to diversity in gender, cultural heritage, colonial histories, ethnicity, class, and sexuality (among others). We no longer focus only or even centrally on static models of matrilineal, patrilineal, and bilateral inheritance and residence. We now explore how kin connections are made meaningful in everyday lives.

The concept of relatedness is key here. Over twenty years ago, anthropologist Janet Carsten (2000) edited a volume on relatedness that places the more static and structured understanding of kinship into a wider social frame of connections. The contributors to this volume consistently and persuasively claim that relatedness encompasses an array of emotional feelings and social standards of family connectedness that include but are not reducible to biological relationships. This approach resonates with and builds upon Carsten's (1995, 223) earlier work with Malays on the island of Langkawi, in which she argues persuasively that "for these Malays, kinship itself is a process of becoming." The meaning of kinship, Carsten continues, cannot be assumed. "Ways of living and thinking about relatedness in Langkawi ... [stress] a processual view of personhood and kinship. It is through living and consuming together in houses that people become complete persons – that is, kin" (224). Relatedness, then, has social and emotional as well as material and behavioural dimensions that must be considered in discussions of family and kin networks. Among the Malays of Langkawi, all of these dimensions are represented through blood, but blood as a physical substance is seen to be just as malleable and flexible as social relatedness:

> It is clear that not only is "social" identity in Langkawi unfixed, but "physical" identity, a person's substance, is also continuously acquired and alterable. Identity and substance are mutable, fluid, and closely connected. Thus the ideas I describe lead me to question the division ... between the "biological" and the "social," between kinship as a biological, genetic, instant, and permanent relationship, and social identity as fluid. In Langkawi, ideas about relatedness are expressed in terms of procreation, feeding, and the acquisition of substance, and are not predicated on any clear distinction between "facts of biology" (like birth) and "facts of sociality" (like commensality). (235)

This is not to say that biological relationships do not figure centrally in some cultural ideals of family. Elizabeth Roberts's (2012) ethnography of assisted reproduction in Ecuador demonstrates that local kinship ideologies centre on genetic reductionism. When Roberts asked women seeking in vitro fertilization treatments if they would ever consider adoption, the women "responded emphatically that an adopted child is 'not of my own blood. Not of my own body'" (167). However, as Carsten (1995) shows, categories of relatedness are much broader in other contexts, extending beyond biological connections.

Teresa Holmes explains that in the early twentieth century, the kinship system of the Luo Peoples of western Kenya was defined by British colonial officials in terms of agnatic descent, where ties are traced biologically through the father's line. This colonial model of Luo kinship persisted and has been reproduced by historians and other researchers over decades. However, "the Luo themselves used less linear and more flexible and encompassing notions of relatedness to construct socially significant identities" (Holmes 2009, 51). The question we ought to ask, then, moves us beyond the dichotomy between biological and social forces. How do the people with whom we partner in our research define and construct relatedness, and what meaning is attached to this notion (Carsten 1995, 236)?

I set out to explore the everyday meanings and reflections on HIV/AIDS, motherhood, and family among women and men at AIDS Saskatoon. While the stories recounted in this book are grounded in this particular local environment, they are stories that have far-reaching relevance. They are stories of family strength despite the ongoing impact of colonial disruptions to traditional lifeways. They are stories of cooperative care and kindness that defy negative stereotypes of "addicts" as selfish and destructive. They are stories of kin-mediated health that involve not only biological connections but the ties among those who share communities, histories, and a similar ethic of care.

Lakota anthropologist Beatrice Medicine (2001, 259) argues that there is no singular "Indian experience" of family (or anything else). However, Medicine also argues that traditional and contemporary Indigenous kinship systems and caregiving networks are, in broad ways, very different from those of European settlers. She cites John Redhorse, a Cherokee social worker, to point out that "Native American extended families differ from their European counterparts which generally define an extended unit as three generations within the same or nearby household. Rather, Native American extended families assume a distinct village-type network construct" (259). In many Indigenous nations, this village-like network serves to hold individuals accountable for their behaviours to the broader community. Early ethnographic accounts of diverse Indigenous communities emphasize the sharing and distribution of food across family networks (Van Stone 1963), reciprocal exchange of material goods and caregiving (Smith 1981), and family-centred housing and interconnected kin units (Sharp 1979). In the pre-reserve period on the northern plains, "Aboriginal bands ... were relatively small, kin-based communities that relied on the unity of their members for survival.... There were a variety of ways that individuals or groups could become members of a band, but what was of particular importance was that these new members assumed some sort of kinship role with its associated responsibilities" (Innes 2010, 28). These responsibilities were learned through example of others as well as cultural storytelling.

Janna Olynick and colleagues (2016) demonstrate that among the Carrier Peoples of northern British Columbia, the telling of stories to guide children in their journeys toward adulthood was once central to traditional nurturance. Storytelling was undertaken by the whole community, including the children, who participated actively. Residential schools disrupted this practice. Families struggled to maintain their connections to traditional lifeways amidst colonial oppression and degradation. Many families succumbed to the struggle and their traditional stories were silenced. "Being stripped of traditional child-rearing philosophies and cultural practices created a void in the minds of those who attended residential schools, leaving them without any knowledge of how to tend and care for their own children" (Olynick et al. 2016, 156). The Western models of nuclear family imposed on Indigenous Peoples were unfamiliar to Carrier parents, particularly former residential school students. After all, "the type of child-rearing practice in residential schools was not adequate and commonly involved physical, sexual, and verbal abuse" (156).

Many scholars argue that traditional kinship and lifeways were "lost" or "killed" by relentless forces of colonialism. The uprooting of Indigenous Peoples from their home lands, the forced removal of children from their families, and the persistent devaluing of Indigenous life caused, and continue to cause, immeasurable damage to Indigenous communities, families, and individuals. However, there is also a burgeoning literature that explores how the enduring strength and resilience of Indigenous Peoples are often engendered and emboldened by family (see Innes 2010, for example). Throughout the AIDS Saskatoon research, the participants spoke repeatedly of strong family ties and an imperative to care for each other. These accounts do not contradict or otherwise lessen stories of intergenerational trauma and structural violence. Instead, they reveal why and how participants recognized and enacted their long-held responsibilities to care for each other and their families even during times of intense struggle, violation, and difficulty. As Isabel put it, "it's just how we've always done it in the Native world. Us mothers, grandmothers, and aunties work special hard at it."

SITUATING MOTHERHOOD

Motherhood is made. Maternity is the biological process that begins when a woman is pregnant. It continues as she gives birth, nurses her infant, and bonds with her child. But motherhood – the socially recognized and institutionally regulated realm of women's child-related roles, responsibilities, identities, emotions, activities, and resources – is culturally, politically, and historically forged. In many ways and in most industrialized societies, motherhood is constructed through Eurocentric patriarchy. It is governed by patriarchal rules and expectations that privilege the professional skills and waged labour of the masculinized public spheres over the reproductive and unwaged labour of the feminized domestic spheres. Patriarchal forces of all kinds – forces wielded by both men *and* women – advance the notion that maternity is central, even essential, to a woman's social purpose. Indeed, it is commonly assumed that "all women naturally know how to mother, and that the work of mothering is driven by instinct rather than intelligence, and developed by habit rather than skill" (O'Reilly 2014, 4). Women's "natural" and "essential" place, it follows, is in the less visible and more private domestic spheres.

As will be discussed in detail in the next chapter, prevailing Western models of motherhood define mothering as an individualized task. Impossibly high standards of "good mothering" are set, demanding that mothers invest more time than their partners or other family members in child care. According to Anne Milan and colleagues (2015, 21), Canadian women who are part of a dual-earner couple and who work full time spend, on average, fifty hours per week on child care. Men with the same working and relationship arrangements spend twenty-seven hours per week on child care. Indeed, across all employment and relationship categories, women invest more time caring for their children than men do. The same pattern holds true for other domestic work.

This "double work day" limits many mothers' employment opportunities, increasing their dependence on intimate partners.

Among women who are employed, even those with high-paying professional careers, motherhood entails a significant economic cost. There already exists a wage gap between men and equally qualified women who do the same work. Carole Vincent (2013, 14) explains that this inequity is exacerbated by the "family gap." Across thirty countries, men aged twenty-five to forty-four with full-time employment make 6.6 per cent more than women. Among workers with at least one child aged fifteen years or less, the gender gap grows to 21.8 per cent. In Canada, where the gender wage gap sits at 6.5 per cent, the family wage gap results in men with children earning 29 per cent more than women with children.

For women whose earnings and financial circumstances already put them close to the poverty line, the economic costs of motherhood often push them over it. Between 1989 and 2012, child and family poverty increased in Canada by 25 per cent, affecting women and children much more than men (Canadian Women's Foundation 2014). Women in poverty have a difficult time securing employment that pays enough for them to care adequately for their children. Taking second and third jobs to make ends meet means that mothers have less time with their children. They are therefore subjected to harsher public rebuke for what is often seen as deficient mothering.

Anthropologists have been at the forefront in advancing intersectional analyses of these economic and social costs. Those who have collectively endured generations of racism, assault, uprootedness, displacement, and discrimination are those who bear the greatest burdens of poverty and ill health. Just as syndemic theory allows us to understand how two or more health-related conditions interact to exacerbate burdens of illness, an intersectional analysis allows us to explore how social and economic disadvantages are exacerbated when racism, sexism, homophobia, and other harmful social forces overlap in people's lives. Leith Mullings (2005, 80) argues that focusing on how these multiple, historical, and contemporary forces intersect "shifts our analysis to racism rather than race, toward gender subordination as well as sex as biology, and to resource distribution as the larger context that constrains and enables what appears as voluntary lifestyle choices."

Indigenous women in Canada (like elsewhere) often find themselves heavily disadvantaged by intersecting forces of discrimination. Jennifer Brant (2014, 11) argues that Indigenous women have been under siege for generations: "The attacks include the Indian Act of 1876, the residential school system, the eugenics movements, the sixties scoop, and the over representation of children in protective services." Memee Lavell-Havard and Jeanette Corbiere Lavell (2006, 192) argue that the situation is particularly acute for mothers: "Given the increased risk of poverty, homelessness, domestic violence/abuse, food shortage, gestational diabetes, HIV/AIDS, and drug and alcohol addictions, it would seem that in comparison to many other occupations, being an Aboriginal mother is possibly one of the most dangerous in Canadian society."

Being a mother living with or affected by HIV/AIDS and its syndemic conditions is a source of hardship and harm for all the women who participated in this research. As the coming chapters lay out, AIDS Saskatoon mothers face all kinds of challenges and fears associated with their health status, including stigma, public criticism, and incapacitating losses. Although they are grounded in local realities, these challenges and fears are similar to those faced by HIV-affected mothers across the world. Surprisingly, though, there has been relatively little attention paid to mothering amidst HIV/AIDS. The majority of the existing literature focuses on maternal-fetal HIV transmission, mothers' disclosure of seropositivity, and reproductive decision-making. Less attention is paid to the interplay between motherhood as a socially constructed category within a broad family context and HIV/AIDS.

The work that does focus more on the broad range of motherhood suggests that HIV-positive women are vigilant about their health "for the sake of the children" (Valdez 2001), protecting their children from social stigma (Murphy et al. 2006), and defending their identities as "good mothers" (Silver et al. 2003). Although relatively small, this body of work indicates that motherhood reduces the harms of HIV/AIDS, motivating women to make health-maximizing choices. However, a paradox exists: "whereas motherhood usually confers normality on women, motherhood exaggerates the deviant status of HIV-positive women ... placing them in a cultural 'double bind'" (Sandelowski and Barroso 2003, 476). Despite the often valiant efforts of HIV-positive mothers to live up to prevailing standards of maternal care, motherhood and HIV/AIDS are seen to be irreconcilable categories. Motherhood is life-giving; HIV is cast as life-taking. Motherhood is culturally associated with responsibility, HIV/AIDS with irresponsibility. Women who occupy both categories as mothers with HIV/AIDS are subject to harsh criticism and marginalization. "When the other moms at [my daughter's] school found out that I got HIV, they started treating me like crap," Lisa recalled. "Even the ones who was once real nice to me. They started acting like I was dirt. Like I was getting them and their kids dirty. Not nothing I did won them back. Nothing."

Addiction and injection drug use exacerbate the already untenable position in which many HIV-affected mothers find themselves. Nancy Campbell, scholar of science and technology studies, argues that at the turn of the twenty-first century, women with addictions in North America were seen as inhuman, supposedly reproducing their inhumanity in their children. The "prevailing logic is that drug-using women cannot govern themselves, and thus produce unruly children who ultimately reproduce an ungovernable society" (Campbell 2000, 139). Campbell's analysis still applies twenty years later. Headlines such as "Motherhood's Last Taboo" (Hrvatin 2019) accompany news articles that continue to cast mothers with addiction as solely and irresponsibly culpable for the illness and difficulties their children encounter. Of course, stemming the incidence of fetal alcohol spectrum disorder (FASD) and neonatal abstinence syndrome (NAS) is critically important. But, in her detailed analysis of drug-related policies, Campbell (2000, 140) persuasively argues that when policy-makers, health care personnel, and many fetal rights advocates deflect responsibility for addiction onto individual mothers, they render the social causes of drug use invisible. When there is no (or little) accounting for the social conditions of addiction, there is no accounting for the social and family networks that offset the negative outcomes of it.

CONCLUSION

Kinship matters. This is a fundamental anthropological claim. It is therefore surprising that, except for some attention to "family dysfunction" (a hangover from the "family configuration model" of addiction that was popular in the mid-twentieth century), families rarely figure centrally within anthropological studies of HIV/AIDS. Reference is sometimes made to family roles, especially maternal roles. But there is little attention devoted to how people talk about family, how they culturally value child care amidst the HIV/AIDS syndemics, or the everyday connections between family life and HIV-related health.

Ellen Block and Will McGrath's (2019) recent work on AIDS orphans in Lesotho is a notable exception. The authors argue that given the high prevalence and mortality rates of HIV/AIDS in sub-Saharan Africa, its effects are inescapable. In Lesotho, HIV infection extends beyond the individual to entire families. It is, Block and McGrath assert, a "kinship disease." I join Block and McGrath in taking what they call a "kinship-first" approach to studying HIV/AIDS. Rather than exploring how the biomedical realities of the virus map onto local social lives, a kinship-first perspective takes the research participants' social lives as "the soil in which HIV/AIDS takes root, permanently altering the landscape. It is the social world where people live and dwell. HIV is merely a part of the terrain" (Block and McGrath 2019, 7).

Despite the vast geographical and cultural distance between Block and McGrath's research site and mine, structural violence and a legacy of devastating colonial policies are the contexts for both projects. However, their focus is on HIV-affected children who now live without parents. My focus is on HIV-affected parents who face living without their children. Whereas the HIV/AIDS epidemic in Lesotho is fuelled by sexual transmission, the HIV/AIDS epidemic in Saskatchewan is fuelled by addiction and injection drug use. And whereas Block and McGrath's analysis centres specifically on the HIV/AIDS epidemic, mine looks at the broader syndemic context as well. Together, though, our research – along with that of others, including Jean Hunleth's (2013, 2017) work in Zambia and Leslie Robertson's (2007) work among Indigenous women in Vancouver's Downtown Eastside – issues a clarion call for kin-centred approaches to HIV treatment, prevention, and support. After all, "AIDS infects families as much as it infects the body" (Block and McGrath 2019, 7).

3

Motherhood

> To make problematic that which is sacred is to understand it as neither natural or given but as a socially constructed reality. Understanding the socially constructed nature of ideas and practices must begin with the recognition that there are alternative ideologies available, no matter how much these may grate against our deepest sense of what is right and natural.
>
> *– Sharon Hays (2007, 418)*

Isabel is a grandmother from a northern Cree community who moved to Saskatoon seventeen years ago to be with her extended family. She cherishes caring for her seven-year-old grandson Mark. Isabel had gained guardianship of Mark through the recommendation of CFS while Mark's mother (and Isabel's daughter), Shauna, was undergoing HCV treatment. The harsh side effects of the treatment in combination with anti-retroviral therapy for HIV were proving to be unbearable for Shauna. For relief, she had returned to injecting opioid drugs. To ensure Mark's safety, he had been placed with Isabel and her husband. Isabel had embraced the opportunity: "It's just who we are. It's what we do.... It's not much different than it ever was. Us doing all we can for all the kids, even the grown-up ones like Shauna."

Mornings at Isabel's house are hectic. Everyone gets up early. Isabel prepares breakfast and lunches, making a fresh batch of bannock (a traditional bread common in many Indigenous communities) to pack in Mark's lunch so that he has "a taste of home" while he is away at school. Isabel's husband hurriedly prepares for work, and her brother and cousins usually come through her kitchen from their nearby homes for morning comradery. "It's busy but it's home." Isabel explained that sending Mark off to school is a "real event." Her cousin, Serena, who lives across the crescent, comes over to join them; "there's a whole group of us watching Mark head off to school, wishing him well, hoping that the day goes real good for our boy."

Our conversation about Isabel's morning took place in the reception area at AIDS Saskatoon while I was folding the monthly newsletter. Isabel took the chair beside me and picked up the conversation from our interview the day before. As with most anthropological research, the interviews in this project ranged from formal question-and-answer formats to informal conversations that arose spontaneously and unfolded with no scripted or guiding questions. I recorded all these interviews. Like the other research participants, Isabel *wanted* her contributions recorded. She kept checking to ensure that the recorder's battery was sufficiently charged and often tapped the recorder, saying, "This is real important!"

As Isabel helped to fold the newsletters and described Mark's daily departure for school, she leaned into me, pressing her shoulder against mine. I would never have noticed such a gesture in any other circumstance, but this time I did. As warm as my relationship with Isabel had become, she and I were not "huggy" (as she called it). She confided to me on several occasions that she would avoid overly affectionate staff members and visitors to The 601: "All that touching and hugging that the White folks like. It's not for me!" When Isabel purposefully leaned into me as we chatted, the gesture was a way for her to recall and physically represent the family solidarity behind Mark's daily departure.

Just over two weeks later, I was once again sitting with Isabel, this time in the upstairs living room at AIDS Saskatoon where there is much more privacy. The relaxed tone of our earlier conversation was gone. She was crying and upset. Because of Isabel's HIV-positive status and her own history of drug use, regular visits from CFS were required to ensure that Mark was safe in her care. Earlier that week, on a cold winter afternoon, the visit came without warning. Knowing that she would be late from work that day, Isabel had confirmed that

Serena would be at her house when Mark returned from school. After arriving home that afternoon, Mark found his uncle and several friends drinking in the back room, and he knew to head over to Serena's place. "When the social workers came to check up on us, Mark was on Serena's stoop kicking at her screen door because she had it latched," Isabel explained.

> They called me, saying "You left him all alone" and "he had no place to go." But none of that was true. My cousin was there, she was just slow to get to the door. But, no. They said he was outside alone, unsupervised, and they said that's, like, neglect. So they just took him away.... When I go to meet with them the next day, they wouldn't even talk to me in private. They stood out in the waiting room ... and right in front of everybody, and the place was real packed too, so right there they told me that they was going to do another home assessment and until that got done and approved, Mark has got to stay in emergency foster care.

Isabel was very nervous about the home assessment because the first one had focused centrally on her HIV status. For the next month, Isabel was wracked with worry about Mark, concerned that he would forget that his family was rooting for him every day, that he would miss the "taste of home" in his lunches, that he would be lonely and afraid. The worry wore on her. Isabel was not eating well, rarely finishing even the modest portions she would take on soul food days. She was not sleeping much. She was suffering, and her friends at The 601 knew it. "She's going through a real tough one," her friend Theresa told me, adding, with a frustrated sigh, "Them's the hills we gotta climb."

After the home reassessment was finally completed, Isabel came into The 601 just before it closed. She begged the staff to let her stay after hours, just for a while. Her words were slurred and her eyes were bloodshot. Isabel had started drinking as soon as the home visit was completed and, after several hours, she headed to The 601 for solace and support. She saw me and described how her fears about the focus on her HIV status were confirmed:

> They go asking me "When did you get HIV?" "How did you get it?" "What are you doing about it?" It was the third degree. They

> asked about my daughter, how often she uses [drugs]. About my cousin, how often she uses. About me, how often I use. They just assumed we are all still using. Well, I'm not. But they just assumed it. And then when I tried to tell them that Mark wasn't left alone that afternoon, that he had my cousin and his uncle there, they just started quizzing me about who had HIV. It didn't make no sense to me so I started crying. They were painting me all wrong. Like a bad drug mother. I'm a good *kohkum* [grandmother]. I'm not like how they were painting it.

The encounter with the CFS staff had upset Isabel to the point that she drank heavily that afternoon, breaking years of sobriety. However, Isabel was more than upset. She was also confused. She told me repeatedly that she did *not understand* how the social workers could conclude that Mark was "left alone" when family members were home. As we left The 601 and I walked Isabel home, she listed off where each relative lived in proximity to her house. Serena, as we know, lived across the crescent; brother Kyle lived right next door; brother Martin lived with cousin Dennis in the nearby cul-de-sac; and dear friend Theresa, an "auntie" to Mark, lived just up the street. Mark's mother, Shauna, would often stay with another friend only a block away. Even though Shauna was not legally permitted to see Mark without supervision, Isabel believed that the rule could surely be broken in the event that Mark needed emergency assistance. And, of course, Isabel concluded as we said goodbye, "There's The 601, not far away. So *how* could Mark be *alone*?" The allegation of neglect in such a context of social and family connections was truly baffling to her.

It might be difficult for some of us to understand why Isabel was so confused. After all, she was the "mother on record," as one of the CFS social workers had called her. Was it not her obligation to be *the one* to greet Mark when he arrived home from school? Does responsibility for Mark not fall primarily to her and her alone? Questions such as these seem natural to many of us. The underlying premise of these kinds of questions, however, is no more natural than Isabel's understanding of motherhood and child care as collective endeavours that involve shared responsibility. Both sets of understandings constitute different models of motherhood born of cultural and political histories. Anthropologists and other social scientists strive to identify and examine the cultural and historical forces that give rise to what is often considered natural. One of our most important goals is to understand how these cultural and historical forces affect the daily lives of those exposed to and entangled by them. This chapter discusses these forces; I ultimately argue that, for the AIDS Saskatoon mothers who participated in this research, any model of motherhood that does not account for the collaborative context of child care undermines their efforts to care for their families and themselves.

INDIVIDUALISTIC MOTHERHOOD AND INTENSIVE MOTHERING

In her fascinating autoethnography of motherhood in Upper East Side Manhattan – a dramatically different cultural context from The 601 – Wednesday Martin (2015) argues that prevailing understandings of what motherhood is, and should be, are tied to contemporaneous understandings of childhood. In most affluent societies today, childhood is a time of protected innocence, child-centred learning, and perceived vulnerability. But it has not always been this way, nor is it currently this way everywhere. Martin (2015, 60–1) argues that "the idea that childhood is a carefree idyll is a modern Western invention that comes [largely] from affluence." Childhood, Martin asserts, did not evolve as a period of precious innocence but as a necessity for adults. In the past, childhood was about work, not play. Evolutionary biologist Barry Bogdin (1997, 63) suggests that human childhood evolved to be of longer duration than that of our primate relatives not only to give children more time to learn aspects of human culture (language, sociality, tool use, and so forth) but also because children were essential helpers to adults, taking care of other youngsters, contributing to food collection, and thereby extending human longevity and reproductive success.

Not only is the carefree idyll of childhood not found in our evolutionary past, it is also not the norm outside of affluent North American and European communities. Children among the hunting and gathering Hadza Peoples of Tanzania, for example, cooperate with all age groups in order to meet important responsibilities for foraging and food provision (Hawkes, O'Connell, and Jones 1995). Suzanne

Gaskins (2003) describes a similar involvement of children in agricultural as well as domestic work in rural Maya villages in the Yucatan peninsula, where children as young as ten instruct and supervise even younger children in various household and farming tasks. These Hadza and Maya communities are similar to other horticultural societies in that children are expected "to participate in the work and routine of the community and are not regarded as requiring special attention or care" (Furedi 2002, 106). In these societies, greater agency and independence are often granted to children who contribute tangibly to the world around them while at the same time being loved and valued by family and friends. Nana Clemenson's (2016) work in the Hang'ombe village in southern Zambia illustrates this well; children's participation in adult life (socializing with adults, contributing to agricultural work, sharing in child care responsibilities) allows them to engage and experiment creatively, playfully, and meaningfully with social roles and conventions.

In contrast, North American childhood today is largely located within a separate social sphere. According to Wedenesday Martin (2015, 60), "Rather than hanging out in language- and skill-rich multi-age groups with lots of older and younger siblings," middle-class and affluent American children are "sequestered from the rest of society with kids their own age.... In our world, kids are *work*, and our lives are arranged around their needs, rather than the reverse." The history that has given rise to this culturally specific view of childhood is marked by urbanization, the rise of industrial global markets, declining fertility, smaller families, the growth of the middle class, and the deepening separation of private and public domains (see Heywood 2013; Lancy 2015).

The changing ways in which personal and cultural risk is understood also contributes to the notion that, today, children are always "at risk," even when that risk cannot be readily identified. Contemporary Western views of childhood are cast in terms of speculative threats, the "what ifs" of life. Children are seen as incapable of navigating their way through these threats without parental, and specifically maternal, guidance: "It is hard to overestimate how far the concept of the 'at risk' child has expanded when applied to the area of parenting. Children are cast as particularly vulnerable in today's culture, with their health and safety seen as compromised by a toxic social environment" (Lee et al. 2014, 44). Indeed, since the mid-twentieth century, terms such as *delicate* and *helpless* have been increasingly used in the descriptions of children that appear in news stories, child-rearing manuals, political discourse, and health care pamphlets (Stearns 2009), underscoring views of childhood vulnerability.

Childhood in affluent and urban North America, then, has undergone a historical shift, from a focus on children's capabilities and family contributions to a preoccupation with children's vulnerability and unique needs. It is not that children were not valued and loved in previous times, nor is it that physical juvenility – the actual biology of being at earlier developmental stages than adults – was not fully apparent in the past. It is also important to note that some children were, and are, made vulnerable by forces beyond their control. These children need protection. But there is now a generalized and sentimentalized depiction of childhood in contemporary North America that is markedly different from the understandings and realities of childhood in other times and other places. This difference, Lee and colleagues (2014, 37) tell us, is "as much about the imagination and action of adults as it is about physical children."

The model of motherhood that emerges from and helps to shape this sentimentalized understanding of childhood has a highly individualized focus. Rather than seeing mothers within broader family and community contexts, the prevailing public, as well as expert, gaze is cast almost always, if not entirely, on the individual women who mother. There have been several terms for this individuation of motherhood. Frank Furedi's (2002) "parental determinism" and "paranoid parenthood," Anette Lareau's (2011) "concerted cultivation," Joan Wolf's (2011) "total motherhood," and Susan Douglas and Meredith Michaels's (2004) "new momism" all refer, with only slight variation, to the intense and narrow focus on individual parents, most commonly mothers, as singularly accountable for the care, nurturing, and protection of children. In the past decade or so, there has been a corresponding proliferation of terms for mothers themselves that describe (often judgmentally) the extent to which each woman is living up to, falling short of, or overstepping her individual responsibilities. Protective "grizzly mothers" (Miller 2010), demanding "tiger mothers" (Chua 2011), and hovering "helicopter mothers" (Stokes 2014) join the emotionally distant "refrigerator mothers" (Kanner 1973) of the mid-twentieth century. With such a strongly individualized focus, the role of mother has become the object of intense scrutiny, arguably more than ever before.

In anthropology, Sharon Hays's (1996, 2007) analysis of what she calls intensive mothering has been among the most influential of such studies. The individualistic model of motherhood gives rise to intensive mothering that, according to Hays (2007, 414), is "child-centred, expert-guided, emotionally absorbing, labour-intensive, and financially expensive." This all-consuming style of mothering leaves little room for the health and self-care of mothers themselves. Just as the once-popular radio talk show host Laura Schlessinger would introduce herself to listeners not by her name but by the phrase "I am my kid's mom," Upper East Side Manhattan mothers, Wednesday Martin (2015, 61–2) notes, refer to themselves exclusively in relation to their children: "We introduced ourselves, or signed off, as 'Pierce's mom' or 'Avery's mom.' These women had become their offspring, and vice versa.... We were our children, utterly merged together."

While women are consumed by the all-encompassing demands of intensive mothering, they must, in turn, consume goods and services in order to live up to the standards that this model of motherhood demands. Fertility treatments, pregnancy services, childbirth coaches, lactation consultants, educational toys, private schools, tutors, extracurricular activities, and professional nannies are part of the vast assemblage of market goods and services that mothers are encouraged to access and manage. Intensive mothering is expensive. Marilisa Racco's (2017) recent *Global News* report puts the costs in Canada at over $250,000 per child. This dimension of motherhood is intensifying quickly: "Consumption and consumer culture shape parenting in ways unimagined even a decade ago" (Demo 2015, 1). Of course, this is part of the contemporary embrace of the social and economic philosophy of neoliberalism. In demanding minimal government involvement in the national economy and heralding individual entrepreneurialism, neoliberalism erodes social welfare supports for families, assigning responsibility for well-being and prosperity to individuals rather than governments. Parents, primarily mothers, therefore must turn to the marketplace for the resources that will enable them to provide and care for their children knowledgably and effectively (Vandenbeld Giles 2014).

Central in the assemblage of goods and services that mothers are encouraged to access is the advice and assistance of experts. Just as intensive mothering is financially expensive, it is also expert guided. Who are these experts? Most certainly, they are those with professional licences to dispense expertise and assess maternal performance, such as health care practitioners, social workers, and counsellors, to name only a few. The field of experts has also expanded to include those with self-proclaimed expertise, often celebrity mothers, who choose to share their maternal journeys publicly.

The ever-growing scholarly literature that examines the child care advice industry reveals some very interesting trends. First, since the mid-twentieth century, kick-started by pediatrician Dr. Benjamin Spock's (1946) best-selling treatise *The Common Sense Book of Baby and Child Care*, popular child care manuals place more demands on individual mothers while minimizing the roles played by other family members and non-remunerated caregivers (Lupton 2011; Marcotta 2009). Second, the use of individualized and often highly stylized case examples has steadily increased, introducing women to expert-endorsed role models to guide their mothering behaviours (Bedor and Tajima 2012; Douglas and Michaels 2004). Third, mothers who do not follow whatever advice is currently in vogue are not seen simply as different. They are seen and treated as potentially dangerous to their children (Ehrenreich and English 1979; Wolf 2011). And, fourth, the marketing of expert advice has expanded considerably. There are now more than twenty thousand books currently in print and over two dozen parenting magazines with a combined circulation of over twenty million (Marcotta 2009, 204). Beyond these publications, the marketing of expert advice figures centrally in parenting classes (Esnard 2015), parenting websites (Gatrell 2011), and the everyday professional practices of health care providers, counsellors, and social workers (Hardyment 2008). As Lee and colleagues (2014, 30) note, there is now "an army of professionals who colonize parenting, as it is increasingly understood to be too important to be left up to parents."

To be fair, there is little doubt that some women find intensive mothering rewarding and life affirming. There is equally little doubt, however, that under even the best of circumstances, even for women who enjoy health and affluence, intensive mothering takes a toll. Psychologist Shari Thurer (1994, xvi) argues that intensive mothering creates an unattainable myth of motherhood that not only raises expectations to the point that it becomes hazardous to mothers' mental health but also "makes a scapegoat of mom; [and] it leads to an over-emphasis on what she does, at the expense of a broader understanding of child development." Academic and popular literature is rife with examples of how mothers who have social privileges of all kinds are struggling under the weight of intensive mothering even as they idealize it (see, for example, Hinton, Laverty, and Robinson 2013; O'Reilly 2006; Vandenbeld Giles 2012). As Thurer (1994, i) cogently notes, "A sentimentalized image of the perfect mother casts a long, guilt-inducing shadow over real mothers' lives," and maternal performance anxiety now reigns supreme.

For Isabel and all the mothers who participated in this research, this individualistic model of motherhood and the intensive mothering it requires are problematic in at least two ways. First, the very association with "the plague of our time" and all that it entails renders mothers with HIV immediately suspect. The research participants consistently described being seen by those around them – neighbours, community leaders, health care providers, social workers, and teachers, among others – not as protective and loving mothers but as "risk factors" to their children. This perception, which in most cases is largely if not entirely inaccurate, casts the women as failing or bad mothers because they are seen to embody the very risk that protective and good mothers should mitigate. Lisa, the woman from a northern Dene community who was introduced in the previous chapter, described how the denigration of her mothering wears on her: "It don't matter what I do right for my kids, or that I love my kids with all my heart, or that they got everything they need. All that seems to matter is that I got HIV and people think I can't be a good mom. That's real hard to take." Isabel's good friend and cousin, Sally, similarly notes that "having HIV means that we're immediately suspected of bad things when it comes to the kids and grandkids. Nobody knows how well I take care of my grandkids because they don't want to know. They have already decided to hate me." I followed up by asking Sally who "they" are. "It's pretty much everybody I got to deal with." Rachel had come into the room when Sally and I were talking and interjected, "And it's not just that they hate us. It's that they're out for us. To judge us hard, and to take our kids."

These sentiments were expressed consistently and repeatedly by all thirty women who participated in this research. They described feeling targeted by an ever-present system of surveillance and judgment in which they are cast as foregone failures as mothers. Frank Furedi (2002) describes this as targeted parental determinism, the perception that certain parents – those who require particular social services such as welfare, rehabilitative health care, employment assistance, and mental health services – pose elevated risks to their children and therefore need ongoing monitoring. Because consideration of mothers' wider contexts of social, family, and community supports are not easily accommodated within the prevailing and individualistic model of motherhood, the women participating in this research find themselves repeatedly accused of being bad mothers regardless of their actual mothering practices. They are, to paraphrase Isabel's astute observation, being painted "all wrong."

Ellie Lee, Jan Macvarish, and Jennie Bristow (2010, 295) draw on Furedi's notion of targeted parental determinism to argue that "the risk that parents present to children is not only considered significant when parents are considered to be 'bad.' Parenting is also problematized when [they] are construed to be 'unaware' or 'out of touch.'" CFS investigations into the fitness of HIV-affected and -infected mothers sometimes include referrals to parenting classes because the mothers are deemed to be ignorant of the risks that they pose to their children. As one social worker with whom I once spoke put it, "My job is to make sure that [the mothers] know better so they can do better. Most of these AIDS moms are just uneducated." The solution to this, of course, is to turn to the experts in order to ensure that parents are equipped with necessary, up-to-date knowledge regarding child care. Ironically, this solution constitutes the second way in which HIV status and vulnerability make the individualistic model of motherhood problematic for AIDS Saskatoon mothers.

The expert advice readily available to the research participants is rarely of direct relevance to their life circumstances given its individualistic focus and the inherent assumptions of maternal well-being, stable and accessible housing, and consistent financial resources. As explained earlier, expert advice to mothers has, since the mid-twentieth century, focused increasingly on individual and mostly middle-class mothers without due attention to the contexts that influence them.

For mothers with HIV, this broader context is of paramount importance. In addition to routine child care, there are medication regiments to follow, appointments to keep, counselling to attend, addictions to manage. These kinds of activities require cooperative and collective efforts that are rarely, if ever, included in the advice on how to mother independently and intensively. The mothers who participated in this research must rely on unremunerated others to help them manage and reduce the HIV-related challenges and harm in their lives. Advice that does not include these helpers misses the mark. Moreover, the representations of affluent and racially privileged mothers that figure so consistently and centrally in expert advice do not represent AIDS Saskatoon mothers. A deep sense of exclusion results and limits research participants' engagement with the expert guidance prescribed by proponents of intensive mothering.

"When I look at that pretty mother on the poster, the one with the white teeth and white skin and white dress and white baby blanket," forty-four-year-old Susan said, pointing at the poster that hung in The 601, "I feel real invisible. I feel like people want to look at her, but nobody wants to look at me, the poor old Native woman with broken teeth and dirty clothes who's always got her street friends around her." Janice responded similarly to a story told in one of her court-ordered parenting classes:

> The teacher told a story about a White girl who was homeless and got up the courage to go back to her parents' place ... because her kid needed better care. It was a real happy ending. There's no happy ending for me. I got taken away from my dad and sent to a foster home in Regina when my mom killed herself and it came out that my uncle had been raping me. I don't got that kind of homecoming in my story.... It all felt pointless. And I felt hopeless. I felt real left out.... All I want is to care for my girls 'cause I *do* know how. But I felt real left out.

Michaela, a twenty-eight-year-old Euro-Canadian woman with an eight-year-old daughter, described similar feelings of exclusion in response to the stories that other women shared in her addictions support group in one of the wealthier neighbourhoods of the city: "None of the other moms have Aboriginal friends. All of my friends are Aboriginal. None of the other moms worry about being homeless. I worry every day that I'll end up on the streets. I felt like the stranger in the room, like I didn't belong there. Like I was the only one with the *really* broken life."

AIDS Saskatoon mothers reported having a hard time seeing themselves in the scenarios and stories included in the programs that they access and in the published and online resources that routinely circulate. This is important because stories generally have persuasive power only when listeners and readers can place themselves in the narrative, when there is resonance with their lives. When motivational speakers share stories of survival or success, for example, they do so with the hope that, in at least some way, the stories could be those of their listeners too. Folklorists and scholars of semiotics refer to the connection between stories and actions as ostension (Dégh and Váazsonyi 1983). In her study of AIDS legends in Newfoundland and Labrador, Diane Goldstein (2004, 30) explains that, in its narrowest sense, ostensive action takes a "copycat" form in which the listener enacts the story exactly as it was told. In a broader sense, ostensive action is indicated by behavioural choices based on knowledge of and identification with a given story. Because the AIDS Saskatoon mothers do not readily identify with the stories that figure in the support programs and expert advice that they encounter, they experience what can best be described as ostensive exclusion. This kind of exclusion is not without consequence. Not only does it exacerbate feelings of isolation and otherness, it leads many AIDS Saskatoon mothers to withdraw from support programs and refuse to make the desired behavioural changes because, in Janice's words, they seem pointless.

This is not surprising. Over twenty years ago, psychologists Penelope Lockwood and Ziva Kunda (1997) found that among university students in Ontario, the use of role models in motivational stories can have a detrimental effect when the role model's achievements are viewed by listeners as unattainable or when there is too much cultural distance between the role model and the listener. Although this finding pertains to a student population quite different from HIV-affected and -infected mothers in Saskatchewan, it has some applicability. The successes and strategies of highly individualized, racially privileged, and middle-class mothers appear to the AIDS Saskatoon moms as unachievable. This is because the stories of successful and intensive mothering rarely involve women who live with the stigma and health challenges of HIV, addictions, and related conditions. It is also because the stories of successful and intensive mothering rarely involve women who face the precariousness of poverty and the realities of racism as most of the AIDS Saskatoon mothers do. Finally and importantly, it is because there is a significant cultural distance between those who embrace the individualistic model of motherhood and those who are alienated by it.

COLLECTIVE MOTHERHOOD: A "*KIKOSEWIN* THING"

Ethnography is as much about attending to the small moments and quiet words as it is about the public events and larger social trends. These small moments can create vantage points through which we can see the broader landscapes of people's lives (Seligman, Wasserfall, and Montgomery 2015). One such moment occurred in 2011 in The 601 when Isabel, Rachel, Sally, and Theresa were sorting through five large bags of newly donated clothes, creating piles of selected items for several PWAS. It was a seamlessly coordinated flurry of activity as the women were checking sizes, folding items, swapping items, reaching over each other, reaching around each other, rearranging the piles, all the while chatting nonchalantly about a television show that was on in the background. I later told Isabel how awestruck I was by their speed and the inherent logic of their sorting technique. She laughed, quietly saying, "It's a *kikosewin* thing."

Kikosewin is a Cree term for being with family. Isabel explained that it means "when you got your people all around. All the people who are your family, your blood and people who are so close to you that they're like blood. It's a feeling and it's a job and it's a home. It's the people who walk with you and who take care of each other." It was with a mutually understood and community-focused sense of family – both The 601 family and their own families – that Isabel, Rachel, Sally, and Theresa were able to sort the donated clothes so quickly, deciding which item should be set aside for whom. In this informal exchange and with few words, Isabel summed up how most AIDS Saskatoon mothers go about caring for their families: "It's a *kikosewin* thing."

Kim Anderson (2000, 2003, 2007), a Cree-Métis scholar of indigenous studies and one of the leading researchers of Indigenous families, argues that despite the rich diversity that characterizes the First Nations in Canada, one of the shared values of Indigenous Peoples across the country is collective caregiving. Many First Nations celebrate and honour their histories of traditional kin-based economies that were sustained by the work of men and women alike. Before the full impact of European colonialism had taken hold, mothers in these traditional societies held considerable economic as well as familial power, living and working in extended family units that precluded the kind of isolation and subordination faced by mothers in many non-Indigenous, settler families. Child care was undertaken collectively in Indigenous communities as mothers and other kin members worked together to nurture, provide for, and protect the children (Anderson 2007, 763). Because it was connected to prevailing understandings of the natural environment, motherhood was also understood in many First Nations as an embodiment of Mother Earth and was consequently a site of reciprocity as well as responsibility: "If mother was to continue to provide, so the logic went, she must be nurtured in return" (Anderson 2007, 766). There were, therefore, strong and mutually reinforcing interdependencies among mothers and other community members not only to care for the children but to sustain connections with the land and to enable communal health as a People.

Although it takes different forms today and although there remains great diversity across First Nations, the collective interdependencies that Anderson describes still very much inform contemporary practices and experiences of Indigenous mothering. In her study of Indigenous women's political movements in Canada, anthropologist Jo-Anne Fiske (1996, 77) argues that "kin ties are evoked as symbols of community and nature; blood and culture, not law, define ethnic identity and citizenship within a Nation that nurtures and sustains [its] people." Mothers are central to this. As in the past, motherhood is an honoured institution and it extends well beyond the individual relationships between mothers and children to the entire community. First Nations mothering is "a social and cultural act that occurs between multiple configurations of people of many generations – individually and communally. Mothering, understood in this way as a complex web of relational practices, was and is fundamental to life" (National

Collaborating Centre for Aboriginal Health 2013, 3). In their study of Indigenous women involved in sex work in four Prairie cities, Sinéad Charbonneau and colleagues (2014, 166) found that mothering entails "taking care of siblings as a child, raising nieces and nephews, grandmothers raising grandchildren, and mothering the whole community. Family is not only about the children that mothers give birth to; family includes the people that truly understand because they have shared experiences and complex empathy." Without doubt, a collectivist ethos prevails.

It is important to emphasize that within this understanding of collective motherhood there is, and always has been, expectations of individualism and individuated responsibility. Equally, within the individualistic model of motherhood there is, and always has been, awareness that children live in communities and families as well as with parents. Yet, while there may be some overlap between these two models, one is defined in contrast to the other. For AIDS Saskatoon mothers, the collective matters more.

Sally, one of the regulars in The 601, is a forty-two-year-old mother of six children and grandmother of four. Originally from a Cree community in southeastern Saskatchewan, Sally grew up in foster homes in Regina before moving to Saskatoon in the mid-1990s. She has a history of injection drug use and lives with HCV and HIV. "My thirteen-year-old daughter, my youngest, she's giving me real trouble," Sally explained. "I thank God that I got a good husband, older kids, Isabel and my other friends here at the 601 to help me carry this kid. I'm not strong enough to take care of her on my own." Sally went on to list a total of fourteen people who routinely join her in parenting her youngest daughter, a girl who Sally believes is "heading for trouble, talking back, smoking, staying out late, and not taking school seriously." Sally's situation is characteristic of almost all of the AIDS Saskatoon mothers. For example, at the time of our interview, Anne – a thirty-eight-year-old woman originally from northern Saskatchewan who, like Sally, has six children – lived with her nineteen- and seventeen-year-old sons, while her three youngest children (aged twelve, ten, and six) lived with her twenty-two-year-old daughter in Alberta. "I'm Métis and I haven't been back to [my home community] in a long time so I don't got a rez family like lots of the girls here do," Anne explained. "But my kids and me aren't alone. Lots of people are here to hold us up when I feel like I'm falling back into the drugs, or when the methadone or the ARTs are making me sick, or whatnot." Raylynne similarly described her "whole hometown" coming together to guide her two young daughters "down the right road so they learn what they need to be good, strong Dene girls and women who don't need to start doing drugs and risking their health to hide from life." Indeed, most of the research participants depicted a cooperative and integrated approach to child care that is reminiscent of traditional Indigenous mothering.

Interestingly, all four non-Indigenous women who participated in the AIDS Saskatoon research also described collective mothering. Sarah, for instance, called her aunt her "sister mommy" because of the collaborative approach they take in caring for her children. Michaela repeatedly noted that only her AIDS Saskatoon friends knew what she was facing as a mother with HIV, and she could therefore always count on her "601 family" to take care of her daughter when she needed them. As a mother who works two jobs while undergoing treatment for HCV, Jennessa also relied on her friends from The 601 when she was too tired and sick to care for her three young children, saying, "The girls here, they don't ask for anything. They just come and pick up the kids, pick up where I left off, pick me up whenever I need them. They're like sisters to me and aunties to my kids." Finally, Kara, a twenty-four-year-old mother who was in the late stages of AIDS and facing the onset of AIDS dementia complex (ADC) when we met, needed the help of her family and community more than ever. Although her narrative was difficult to follow, Kara described with reasonable clarity how she envisioned her death: "With my 601 family around me. Holding me. Drumming and singing.... Loving my boy like he was blood." Although they do not share the Indigenous heritage of the other research participants, these four women embrace a similar and collective approach to mothering that allows them to meet the needs of their children despite the challenges that HIV presents.

Just as intensive mothering relies on a culturally specific view of childhood and children, so too does collective mothering. There is far greater emphasis put on both children's independence and integration in models of collective motherhood. Children are encouraged to take on their responsibilities to their families, communities, schooling, and themselves with guidance but not constant direction from parents and kin. They are not sheltered from adult life but, rather, included in it. All of the research participants agreed that children's safety and well-being were a top priority in their lives, but children's unfettered integration into community life and enabling children's abilities to act independently held a central place in the participants' interviews as well. Anne trusts her twenty-two-year-old daughter with her younger children because "the kids get all the love and protection they need but they also got to figure some things out for themselves. They got to be a part of [my daughter's] life, not left out of it." Indeed, the obligation to keep children safe but not separate was emphasized consistently and repeatedly by all research participants.

In regard to HIV/AIDS, the integration of children into adult life means that they often learn about the condition from their everyday interactions in their community, as well as from formal educational sources. "The kids all know about HIV and Hep," Sally explained. "I don't hide that from them or nothing like that. There's no way that I'd let them do drugs around me. But drugs, HIV, and Hep, they're a part of life and the kids better know how to get along in a world that has got these things in it." Interestingly, the majority of the online resources targeted specifically to HIV-positive parents focus heavily on the strategies for disclosing HIV status to children (see Brewer 2016). However, these resources are rarely used by AIDS Saskatoon mothers. The risks and realities of HIV are not hidden from their children, who learn about the HIV status of their loved ones through daily medication routines, social work visits, comradery in The 601, and other regular occurrences in the lives of the research participants and their families. "I don't remember telling or teaching Mark about HIV," Isabel explained, "he just kind of figured it out 'cause of his mom's reactions to ART and seeing me put my meds schedule on the fridge. There was no drama about it or nothing like that."

Collective motherhood and the emphasis on children's independence and integration into adult life, however, have drawn harsh judgment. Children's independence and autonomy are often misinterpreted as problematic behaviours resulting from overly permissive, lax, and even neglectful mothering (Johnston 1983). Kin-based collaborative child care is often misrepresented as a lack of parental fitness. These misrepresentations come at a great cost. Recall Rachel's comment that neighbours and service providers "judge us hard, and ... take our kids." Although the judgment that AIDS Saskatoon mothers face is exacerbated by their HIV status and risk, similarly harsh judgments befall others as well. The case of Joann-May Cunday, a Cree mother from Manitoba who moved with her boyfriend and two children to Sherbrooke, Quebec, is a particularly stark example of how this judgment bears on mothers who do not adhere to intensive mothering. According to Cheryl Gosselin (2006), Cunday's boyfriend accused her (falsely, as it turned out) of being a "bad mother" in retaliation for her charges against him for abuse. Citing from the records of the Human Rights Tribunal that Cunday later launched for reparation, Gosselin (2006, 200) describes what happened during the investigation into Cunday's maternal fitness:

> At one home visit ... the social worker believed the kids to be "misbehaving." When Cunday tried to explain that raising children was done differently in Indigenous cultures, the social worker told her "that [her lifestyle] was not the way that people lived in Quebec and that discipline was important".... At a later court proceeding in Youth Division, the social worker said to Cunday, in front of her lawyer, that "if she wanted to adopt the Indian way of life, she could go and live in the north where they have no rules or regulations and let their kids run wild."

Joann-May Cunday's case represents the clash between individualistic and collective motherhood. Priority is given to individualistic models of motherhood in virtually all political and health care contexts, so much so that by the mid-1990s, social service policies across North America had shifted from providing resources to mothers in diverse situations (poor mothers, Indigenous mothers, mothers with disabilities, mothers with HIV) to providing resources to bring diverse parenting practices into conformity with intensive mothering (Connolly 2000, 269). There is, therefore, a colonizing nature to the politics of individualistic motherhood. It is considered to be the best model of motherhood. Deviations from this model are seen as failures that must be corrected and subjected to state oversight.

Indigenous mothers are made particularly vulnerable by the colonizing effects of intensive mothering and its advocates. We are at a point now, Sinéad Charbonneau et al. (2014, 173) tell us, where "the role of extended kinship relationships in raising children in Indigenous communities is largely unrecognized by child welfare systems in Canada." The more that women depart from intensive mothering, the more surveillance they draw. Randi Cull (2006, 153) explains that all too often "Aboriginal mothers live their lives under a state-controlled microscope and no one's life or behaviours look acceptable under that type of unnatural and unjust scrutiny."

There is, of course, a long history to state-sponsored scrutiny and surveillance of Indigenous women in Canada. As discussed in the introductory chapter, residential schools were established by the Canadian federal government and religious institutions to force diverse Indigenous Peoples to assimilate with the English and French colonial societies. First Nations and Métis mothers were often singled out by Indian Affairs agents and Euro-Canadian religious leaders as being deficient: too lax and neglectful. This provided justification for the children to be apprehended and sent off to residential schools where girls were taught to be domestic workers and boys were trained in farming and trades (Miller 1996). The accusation that Indigenous mothers were "unfit" has, in many ways, endured even as the residential school era and sixties scoop policies recede into history. This is "a deleterious stereotype that continues to justify inappropriate and unjustified state intervention into the lives of Aboriginal women" (Cull 2006, 153).

For Indigenous women living with HIV and addiction, the vulnerability to allegations of being unfit mothers is heightened, and the surveillance and intervention seem unending. As a survivor of the Prince Albert Indian Residential School, Isabel lamented that "since coming for us and putting us in residential school, they just don't let us be. It's the reason that we're all suffering so bad now." Rachel agreed: "My grandmother tried to hide my mom so [the government agents] wouldn't take her to the residential school so far away. But they found her. My mom was hurt real bad and then drank her life away. Now they're coming for my kid. It don't stop. I know I need help getting better, getting off drugs, but help sure as hell isn't going to come from snatching up my kid. That'll just make it worse for me and for [my son]." Like Isabel and Rachel, twenty-two other research participants referenced the history of residential schools and the sixties scoop as they spoke about their fear and distrust when service providers (of all kinds) focus on their mothering practices. They argue that HIV is now the new "witch hunt" that allows government agencies to extend the legacy of apprehending Indigenous children because of the misrepresentations of the collective ethos of Indigenous motherhood. As Sally stated during our last interview, "The war is still on."

The stories of residential school and sixties scoop survivors resonate with the research participants in ways that the stories of intensive mothering do not. There is, therefore, an ostensive response by the AIDS Saskatoon mothers to these stories of child apprehension. They do not seek out or rely on expert advice regarding the care of their children for fear that their children will be taken from them. Instead, they rely on their family and communities of support for guidance and assistance, reinforcing the model of collective motherhood.

Collective motherhood not only prevails in Indigenous and HIV communities but is embraced in other North American contexts as well. Annette Lareau (2011) documents that among working-class and poor families in the United States, collaborative child care is far more frequent than the relegation of responsibilities to individual mothers. This holds true in many African American communities (Jarrett, Jefferson, and Kelly 2010), as well as among lesbian mothers (Gibson 2014), mothers of children with disabilities (Jenks 2005), rural mothers (Sutherns and Bourgeault 2008; Walker and Manoogian 2011), and some middle-class mothers, supposedly beacons of individualistic motherhood, who work for wages outside the home (Guerrina 2014), among many others. In these circumstances, as in Indigenous communities, collective motherhood allows parents to care adequately and lovingly for their children while also reaffirming their place and role in a broader kin network and community. As Hillary Clinton (1996) pointed out in the book that she wrote while serving as First Lady of the United States, "it takes a village" to raise a child.

CONCLUSION

A central task of anthropology is to explore how that which is often taken as natural is in fact socially constructed and that which is taken as uniform is in fact politically provisional and culturally varied. I have engaged in this task by arguing here that the often taken-for-granted and highly revered model of individualistic motherhood, and the intensive mothering practices and understandings of childhood that accompany it, are in fact culturally and historically specific. Other models of motherhood and childhood are found elsewhere. In the Indigenized context of HIV in Saskatchewan, collective motherhood has deep roots, but it is often in conflict with individualistic motherhood. The dichotomy between these two models manifests itself in more than ideological differences. For AIDS Saskatoon mothers, there are material and health-related consequences to the colonizing effects of individualistic motherhood. After temporarily losing guardianship of Mark, Isabel was so devastated that her health suffered. Inadequate attention to her diet, anxiety-induced insomnia, and the use of alcohol to numb her pain (one of the only coping mechanisms she has ever found effective) exacerbated the negative side effects of her ART medications, making her so sick that she lost almost a week of work. Those lost wages meant that she could not buy groceries, and without the right food her diet would continue to suffer. The cycle of HIV-related ill health was starting to encircle and close in on her. Luckily, the same kin network that had been in place for Mark on the afternoon of the visit from CFS was in place for her. Serena stocked her cupboards. Rachel visited every night so that she would not be tempted to drink out of loneliness. Theresa cleaned her house. Sally did her laundry. Shauna visited as often as possible. Michaela met Isabel in The 601, where there was coffee, comradery, and laughter.

Despite intense colonial opposition to Indigenous forms of collective motherhood, and despite harsh public judgments of HIV-affected mothers who rely on collaborative child care, collective caregiving has prevailed. It is often a source of great community and kin-based strength even as it is politically overshadowed by individualistic models of motherhood. However, in casting collective motherhood as a positive cultural resource in the lives of AIDS Saskatoon mothers, I share Kim Anderson's (2007, 775) concern that we "run the risk of heaping more responsibility on already overburdened mothers.... Indigenous ideologies of mothering might rightly be accused of creating 'intensive mothering,' Indian-style, if we do not remember some of the fundamental principles involved." These principles include reciprocity and responsibility, taking care of mothers and other caregivers as well as the children. In the context of HIV, these principles include those of harm reduction, forgiving lapses in addiction recovery, and facilitating rehabilitation. They include pride in surviving and thriving: "It is our shared experience of exclusion from society that provides a fertile ground for the revitalization and maintenance of empowering mothering practices" (Lavell-Harvard and Anderson 2014, 2). Honouring these principles of collective motherhood rather than imposing standards of individualistic motherhood would likely be of great benefit to all HIV-infected and -affected mothers, especially those of Indigenous heritage.

With the care and help of those around her, Isabel grew stronger. Three months after Mark had been removed from her home, she had a meeting with two CFS social workers. When I asked about it later, she shrugged her shoulders and said, "It went ok I think. But I really don't want to get my hopes up. If they [CFS] want, they can look real close and see stuff that isn't there." Two weeks later, I was working in one of the upstairs offices of AIDS Saskatoon when the laughter drew me down to The 601. Mark had come home that afternoon and Isabel was eager to share the good news with her friends and family. A celebration had begun. Sally was hugging Mark and Isabel had one hand on Mark's back while she wiped her tears of joy away with the other hand. Isabel's husband came in with boxes of doughnuts and Theresa followed with a freshly made jug of Kool-Aid. People began simultaneously embracing Mark. Within moments the hug was five people deep. Isabel, generally not one to show affection publicly, joined in and then waved me over. "A group hug!" I said in incredulity. "A *kikosewin* hug," Isabel corrected.

4

Fatherhood

> We must ask ourselves: Where are the men?... What are [they] providing for mothers and mothering women as they work through their onerous duties?
>
> – *Kim Anderson (2007, 775)*

It had been a busy and loud afternoon in The 601. The monthly bingo game had drawn a big crowd. Rachel's voice pierced through the din of the television and the various conversations, "Why don't you guys stop jawing away and go talk to her about it, already? She's standing right over there." Four men had been discussing the research recruitment poster. I asked them if they had any concerns or questions: "I'd be happy to pour some coffee and talk about it." Dennis was the first to take me up on it. As he was one of the PWAS who was a member of the CAC that guided the project, Dennis and I had a good working relationship. "I didn't think about this before, but what about us fathers? We got HIV and we got kids and maybe we should be in this project, too." Rachel's brother, Doug, with a naturally booming voice and an ever-present smile, concurred, saying, "I love my kids and I try real hard to make sure that everyone does right by them. But nobody ever asks about being a dad with a big family all around, but I think it's real important." Kyle agreed, "That would be interesting." Tyler was the most reserved and concerned. He leaned against the wall with his arms folded and his head back. "You don't think we got nothing to say about our kids' moms?" Before I could respond, Dennis continued, "We could talk about being fathers and grandfathers and about life with the mothers. You know, from our own perspective." Kyle repeated, "Now *that* would be interesting."

Fathers are a key part of the kin-based circles of care on which AIDS Saskatoon mothers rely. In hindsight, it made good sense to include them in the research, and Dennis, Doug, Tyler, and Kyle presented an important opportunity to do just that. In their own way, they raised the question that Virginia Dominguez (2016, 14), former president of the American Anthropological Association, would ask seven years later: "When we talk more to some people than to others or we find ourselves deeming some people to be more trustworthy [and knowledgeable] than others, are we not participating in the social setting in ways that carry ethical as well as epistemological implications?" In this case, excluding fathers from the study would have belied the principles of partnership and inclusivity that were established with AIDS Saskatoon at the beginning of the project.

Fortunately, more than most other types of research, ethnography can accommodate changes demanded by fieldwork encounters even after the research is underway. Initial findings can be so unexpected that research questions must be revised. Field sites can change suddenly and dramatically. Local political influences can alter investigative efforts. Participants can reshape the project with their varying levels of interest and engagement. As Adam Benkwitz (2016, 5) explains, "A set of problems may be identified before research begins and a general framework may be followed, but it is important for the researcher to remain flexible within an unpredictable natural setting." Rising to this challenge, the CAC supported the addition of a research question that allowed twenty-three fathers to participate: In the Indigenized context of HIV/AIDS in Saskatchewan, how do mothering and fathering influence each other?

FATHERING, FATHER ABSENCE, AND "DOING FATHER TIME"

The scholarly literature on fatherhood and fathering is considerably smaller than that on motherhood and mothering. Historian John Demos famously noted that "fatherhood has a long history but virtually no historians" (LaRossa 1997, 3). The same holds true in anthropology. Using two anthropology-specific library databases, I found over eight thousand more journal publications on motherhood than on fatherhood. Despite this relative paucity, the existing literature on fathering shows considerable cultural variation. Barry Hewlett's (1991, 2001) work on fatherhood among the Aka, a nomadic Mbenga people of the Western Congo Basin, is among the best known. Aka fathers take a central role in caring for infants and children, often carrying and holding them for longer periods of time than mothers and grandmothers do. Bronislaw Malinowski (1929), one of the founders of anthropology, set the groundwork for Hewlett's study in his research among the Trobriand Islanders of Papua New Guinea. Due to the matrilineal structure of Trobriand society, the adult male most central in children's lives is their mother's brother. As a result, fathers must demonstrate commitment to their affinal families (families established through marriage) by caring publicly, frequently, and affectionately for their children, even when biological paternity is not culturally acknowledged. Margaret Mead's (1935, 1938) classic work with the Arapesh peoples of the mountainous regions in Papua New Guinea is similarly foundational in that she aligns fatherhood closely with motherhood. "Among the Arapesh," Mead (1935, 259–60) argues, "both men and women display a personality that, out of our historically limited preoccupations, we would call maternal in its parental aspects."

The fathers in these cultural contexts are in stark contrast to fathers elsewhere. In many societies, there are strong postpartum taboos that prevent men from holding or even seeing their newborn infants. Among the Kipsigis of Kenya, the father's masculinity is thought to be too overpowering for an infant to bear (Harkness and Super 1991). Traditional Han men in China are often deemed inherently incapable of child care and viewed as sources of potential harm to their children (Jankowiak 2011). Yanomamo men in South America, like Kwara'ae men in the Solomon Islands, rarely hold their infants for fear of the polluting effects of urine and feces (Lancy 2015). In some cases, such as among the Yoruba in the Republic of Benin, fathers may be frequently absent, having very little, if any, contact with their children (Semley 2011). In his award-winning ethnography of life among drug dealers in East Harlem, Philippe Bourgois (2003, 292) posits that the distant relationships many fathers have with their children are the consequence of unpaid child support, as well as sexist attitudes and, in some cases, violent behaviour toward the mothers of their children. In contrast to the men in their grandfathers' generation, the young Puerto Rican and Central American men who participated in Bourgois's work in *el barrio* are often absent from their children's lives.

Father absence has drawn considerable scholarly attention since the 1960s, when political concerns about the effects of fatherlessness were coming to the fore in North America (Lamb 2000). While studies of motherhood have long focused on the complexity of mothering practices, studies of fatherhood have taken a more binary approach, exploring the presence or absence of fathers. In the last thirty years, however, there *has* been more diversity in the literature. Attention to "nurturing fathers" (Shirani, Henwood, and Coltart 2012), "intimate fathers" (Dermott 2008), "present fathers" (Krampe and Fairweather 1993), and "involved fathers" (Sayer 2005) complements the work on intensive mothering. Still, the focus on absent fathers remains common, especially in the literature on HIV/AIDS and fatherhood.

The majority of work on fathering in the context of HIV/AIDS centres on the world's "AIDS orphans" crisis. According to the World Health Organization (2014), almost eighteen million children worldwide have been orphaned by the HIV/AIDS pandemic. Scholarly and public representations of the crisis often feature fathers who reject their mother-orphaned children out of fear that they, too, have HIV (Mashegone and Mohale 2016). Other fathers reportedly deny the existence of HIV/AIDS to justify absenting themselves from their children's HIV-related health care (Coertze, Kagee, and Bland 2015). The price of father neglect and absence is high. Children whose fathers are absent and whose mothers have died of AIDS-related causes are less likely to finish basic-level schooling (Nyamukapa and Gregson 2005) and more likely to experience sexual assault and abuse (Kidman and Palermo 2016). There are also far-reaching socio-economic implications for the future of countries, regions, and even continents when the health, educational attainment, and impoverishment of millions of orphaned children are worse than in the generations preceding them (Beegle, DeWeerdt, and Dercon 2009, 561). Local political and cultural alliances are unravelling in ways that gravely concern community leaders and government officials. Throughout sub-Saharan Africa, for example, dying mothers and overwhelmed grandmothers are placing children with matrilineal kin, defying cultural traditions and disrupting generations-old patterns of patrilineal inheritance and patrilocal residence (Ruby et al. 2009). In these cases, father absence and HIV/AIDS are held equally culpable for the shifting cultural tides that many believe threaten community cohesion and economic survival. The general picture of paternal care in the context of HIV is, therefore, a dismal one. There is little resemblance in these depictions to the nurturing fathers that Barry Hewlett and others describe. There is also little resemblance to the fathers who participated in this research.

From the very beginning of the AIDS Saskatoon project, it was clear that fatherhood holds a central place in the lives of most of the men who frequent The 601. They are not always biological fathers to the children in their care. They are uncles, cousins, brothers, and stepfathers, but they take on a paternal role and identify as fathers. They are often not the primary or custodial parent, but they do their best to provide for their children. The relationship Dennis had with his then twenty-four-year old son, Jordan, exemplifies this well.

> He's my son. I call him my son. He was my sister's son. But he's my son now. My sister, Darla, and me, we were living in Edmonton and she died of a cocaine overdose.... I went to court to get custody of this boy because my younger sister, Michelle, was dealing with serious drug problems, too. My other sister, Maureen, wanted custody of Jordy but she was here [in Saskatchewan] and there was too much red tape province to province. It would have taken at least six to nine months for Maureen to get custody of him.... I was already in Edmonton and had a good relationship with [the child care workers] who knew to bring Jordy to me whenever Darla got arrested or was in the hospital. I love being his father.

Dennis's voice grew soft and tears of pride filled his eyes as he talked about Jordan. "He's well mannered and well behaved. And he's never been to jail. Not even once. I'm real proud of that."

Dennis's reference to jail is significant. It is difficult to discuss fatherhood with men who live with addictions and HIV/AIDS and not also talk about incarceration and conflict with the law. The terrain that the research participants navigate every day is highly criminalized because of their past or current drug use, as well as their association with what is often seen as the malevolent transmission of HIV. Hayley Parker (2016, 108) explains, "Though there are no HIV/AIDS specific laws in Canada, individuals may be prosecuted for transmission or non-disclosure of HIV status under [other] laws. Criminalization of HIV implies that HIV infected people are untrustworthy or intent on spreading [the virus]. In this way, they are seen to be monsters out to infect as many people as possible." According to Doug, "Nobody who does drugs and risks HIV is 'off the radar.' You always know that there's a cop or law-abiding finger-wagger waiting to take you down."

The situation is especially acute for First Nations and Métis men. They not only have more frequent encounters with the criminal justice system but are also subject to over-policing and harsher treatment in the courts. The Office of the Correctional Investigator (2013) indicates that Canada's incarceration rate for Indigenous adults is roughly ten times that of non-Indigenous adults. Between 2005 and 2013, the federal Indigenous inmate population increased by 43.5 per cent compared to the 9.6 per cent increase in non-Indigenous inmates. As a result, First Nations and Métis men are significantly overrepresented in penitentiaries across the country, including the Saskatchewan Penitentiary, where they make up 64 per cent of the inmates. Fifteen of the twenty Indigenous men and two of the three non-Indigenous men who participated in this research have been among them at some point. Dennis served time for breaking and entering as well as drug-related offences. He deeply regretted the five months he was away from Jordan while incarcerated. "I'm not a deadbeat dad," he said emphatically. "I wanted to be with him so bad. Jordan was just a teenager and he needed his father."

Dennis also regretted being estranged from his daughter when she was young, long before Jordan came into his life.

> When I broke up with [my first wife], she left our daughter with me. I took her to Prince Albert and then her mom made the stupid mistake of coming to see her, and she ended up taking her to Kelowna [British Columbia], and then she ended up getting strung out on heroin and then she ended up losing custody of [our daughter]. Then I ended up in jail 'cause I was so messed up over that.... I got a letter from social services in BC asking me to

> sign the papers to ok my daughter's adoption by a young couple. I just sent the papers back. I didn't sign them. It just didn't feel right. But time passed and my girl was adopted out while I was in jail. It still feels like a knife in my heart. She and me talk a bit now. I got to meet her kids, my grandchildren. But.... It's just not what I feel like it should be.

Dennis's absence from his children was court ordered and deeply upsetting. It was not reflective of the kind of wilful rejection that frames the depictions of fathers of orphaned African children. "It's like there's a jail culture for us Native guys," Tyler explained, "and we gotta be away from our kids and our kids' mom. We're not just jamming out."

After gaining custody of Jordan, Dennis promised to help him live a different life. "I said to him over and over: 'This isn't going to happen to you.'" Children of incarcerated parents are more likely to be incarcerated themselves (Ng, Sarri, and Stoffregen 2013), and breaking this pattern is extremely difficult amidst the poverty and cultural marginalization that often facilitate criminal activity. It is, however, a challenge that the majority of the AIDS Saskatoon fathers consistently identified as central to their paternal role. "When I look back on my life, I'll know that I've been a good father if my kids stay out of jail," Doug explained. "Their mom and the rest of the family does their thing for the kids. Everybody's got a job. Keeping them out of jail is mine." Ben is a fifty-one-year-old father of two who described himself as "Scotch-Irish-Canadian" and, with a drinking motion, humorously added, "but mostly cheap scotch." He agreed that teaching children to stay "on the straight and narrow" is a job for fathers more than mothers, explaining, "We lay down our own law so the kids don't cross the law of the street or break the cops' law. Mothers can't lay down the law like we can. Fathers got to take that on." For Ben, this meant setting rules, sticking to them, and not "falling for the kids' puppy dog pleading." He added, "It's tougher for the Native guys. They got the world stacked against them."

All of the Indigenous men who participated in this research indicated that keeping children out of the criminal justice system was particularly important for First Nations and Métis families. As Raymond Corrado and colleagues (2014, 45) point out, Indigenous young offenders are almost eight times more likely to be incarcerated than their Euro-Canadian counterparts. They are more likely to be held in the most restrictive type of custody and their sentences are longer, even for the least serious offences. The research participants are well aware of the different realities that their children face in comparison to Euro-Canadian youth. According to Doug, "there is a justice system sinkhole and it's the Aboriginal kids who get pushed and pulled into it more than other kids." Kyle described this most forcefully: "I didn't want [my son] doing the [stuff] that I did. Robbing [convenience stores] for money for [drugs]. Getting into fights. Going to jail.... When White boys pull shit, like doing drugs and fighting, it's called 'acting out.' It's chalked up to 'experience' and they grow up to be lawyers. When Indian boys pull shit like that, they get thrown away and they grow up to be dead."

For the Indigenous research participants, then, the stakes in keeping their children out of the criminal justice system are seen to be life and death. They are stakes that Kyle took seriously, requiring a uniquely paternal response. "Would I ask the kids' mothers to help keep them out of trouble? No, not really," Kyle reflected. "Mostly I'd call on my brothers and cousins. I'd call on them for sure."

This kind of separation of fathering and mothering is expected and accepted by many of the women who participated in this research. As described in the previous chapter, Sally was worried about her teenaged daughter who was "heading for trouble." Sally listed a total of fourteen people who were central in her daughter's upbringing, including her husband, Thomas. "He is the best father I could have ever wanted for that kid," she declared. "He has our help, but he's the one I trust to keep her from running with the wrong pack, to keep that bad-news boyfriend away, and to keep her from ending up behind bars." Unlike Sally, Michaela was generally very critical of her daughter's father but she conceded, "I don't really worry about [my daughter] getting into drugs or getting HIV or getting into gang trouble or going to [a detention centre] like I did. At least when it comes to this, her dad is on the job.... That's the one thing I know I can leave to him. At least he's manning up to do that."

Fatherhood shapes and is shaped by cultural constructions of masculinity. Men rely on what Andrea Doucet (2007) calls the "resources of masculinity" to carve out paternal roles, often in contrast to maternal roles. Although these resources usually refer to the dynamics of race, class, and sexuality, they also entail traits that are culturally valued as virtues in child care (Ross 1994). Strength, protectiveness, and determination are among the traits most readily adopted by men who live in the criminalized context of HIV and addictions. Surviving jail is seen by the research participants as proof that they embody these qualities and are committed to what Dennis called "father time." "Sure, some days when I'd be real pissed off at Jordy for whatever, I'd think of throwing in the towel," he admitted. "But then I remembered what it was like in jail. As a Native guy with HIV, with hepatitis C, with tracks on my arm. And no. No way could I leave him to get sucked into that. That's not what a father does. That's not what a man does. You just gotta be there. You gotta do some serious father time." The men who participated in this research were not always successful in keeping their children out of the criminal justice system or protecting them from harm. Some stories had tragic endings. However, dedication to fatherhood proved to be an important incentive for the men to stay connected with family and to care for the mothers of their children.

The distinction between fathering and mothering that emerges in relation to keeping children out of the criminal justice system is drawn in other areas of child care as well, although rarely with the same precision. Providing emotional comfort, preparing meals, and overseeing body care are parenting tasks in which fathers and mothers engage together but that they approach differently. "Thomas will feed the kids, for sure," Sally explained, "but he feeds them fast food crap. I'm the one that cares more about what they eat." Although Isabel described her husband as "a wonderful grandfather," she was adamant that he not take responsibility for Mark's body care. "I don't know why that kid doesn't like to brush his teeth, but he doesn't! [My husband] lets him [get] away with it. Not me. And haircuts! Did you see that haircut that [my husband] let Mark get? That Mohawk cut? No way would I have let him get it. All that stuff should be left to me and the aunties." Although he prides himself on his friendly and affectionate manner, Doug described his sister and his wife as more capable of providing emotional comfort to his children when they need it: "I don't handle it good when the girls start crying. So, I leave the hugging for the mom, the aunties, and the *kohkums*."

It is interesting that in my observations of The 601, I noted that roughly half of all interactions participants had with their children did not fully align with what they described in the interviews. For example, at one of the monthly soul food lunches, Doug's youngest daughter dropped her dessert on the floor and burst into tearful wails. Doug picked her up and gently rocked her while Rachel brought her another piece of cake. On a separate occasion, Sally's daughter brought her "bad-news boyfriend" into The 601 and it was Sally, not Thomas, who angrily drove the young man away, loudly scolding her daughter for associating with him. The distinctions that were drawn between mothering and fathering, therefore, reflect how the research participants understand their respective parenting roles. Motherhood and fatherhood are cast as somewhat separate but culturally complementary sites within a broader and collective system of child care. However, these distinctions do not always correspond to the everyday activities that mark the participants' parental lives. As Fiona Shirani and colleagues (2012, 37) conclude in their study of fatherhood in Wales, "In highlighting the perceived divergence in men's and women's experiences there is a danger of overstating gender differences ... the connectedness of mothering and fathering is also paramount."

One of the main areas that was identified as a point of strong connection between mothering and fathering is in protecting families and children from the stigma of HIV and addictions. For Doug, "loving the kids isn't enough. It's *work.* Working to keep the haters away, the ones who tell [the children], 'your mom and dad are AIDS junkies and you're shit.' We gotta work hard so the haters don't leave no mark on the kids. It's the work of love."

THE STIGMA, THE SYNDEMIC, AND THE "WORK OF LOVE"

It is not difficult to encounter the widely held assumption that mothers and fathers who are living with or affected by HIV/AIDS and addictions cannot be good parents. I have been confronted by this assumption many times. After asking about my work, a talkative seatmate on an airplane declared that "those junkies have *no right* having children because the kids will grow up to be beasts like their parents." A university administrator told me that the focus of my research was misguided: "You *should* be investigating what can be done for the poor babies, not wasting your scarce research time on the sick parents," she admonished. A student in one of my courses asked, quite nonchalantly, "How many times have you seen AIDS addicts beat their kids to death?" These are not exceptional or isolated examples. HIV and addictions workers have encountered similar sentiments for decades. Almost twenty years ago, sociologist Susan Boyd (1999, 10) explained that "it is assumed that addicted parents fail to protect their children from harm, and that the home environment is characterized as disruptive, chaotic ... and abusive." Add in the confounding forces of HIV/AIDS, and those assumptions intensify.

There is a growing body of work that proves these assumptions false. In a widely respected study, Mary Ellen Colten (1982) compares 170 women in treatment for heroin addiction to 175 demographically similar but non-drug-using women. Colten finds no difference between the two groups in the expression of commitment to their children or in the kinds of child care activities they undertake each day. One of the only differences to emerge indicates that, contrary to assumptions of abuse, the mothers in treatment for heroin addiction use *less* physical discipline than the non-drug-using mothers (89). Barbara Sowder and Marvin Burt (1980) offer similar findings from a study across five major urban centres in the United States comparing 160 families in which there is parental heroin use to 160 families in which there is no drug use. No differences are reported between the two groups regarding child-rearing practices, severity of discipline, reports of neglect or abuse, parental expectations of children, children's attitudes toward school, reports of children ever using cigarettes, or reports of children ever using alcohol. A more recent study employs a three-way comparison among low-income families with regular parental drug use, low-income families with no reported drug use, and middle-class families with one parent serving in the Australian Defence Force (Banwell and Bammer 2006). Once again, no differences in child outcome or parental competence are found. Drawing on a multitude of other studies, as well as their own research with ninety women who are HCV-positive and who have a history of injection drug use, Anna Olsen and colleagues (2014) conclude that parental drug use "should not automatically be associated with an inability to make informed health care choices or to care for children." Instead, they argue that programs "to reduce barriers to obtaining free, non-discriminating reproductive advice and parenting assistance would better utilize women's agency to improve their health."

Unfortunately, the largely erroneous assumptions of parental misconduct among HIV-affected and drug-using parents have persisted despite evidence to the contrary. This is significant in at least two ways. First, these assumptions are self-perpetuating. Linda Nielson (1999, 121) explains that "we generally tend to be on the look-out for and to remember those characteristics that we have been taught to believe are representative of given groups.... [We] seek out 'evidence,' invent 'facts,' and remember the incidents that support whatever beliefs we had about each group to begin with." It is, therefore, extremely difficult to challenge discriminatory assumptions when they are so strongly rooted in well-established cultural bias. Second, these assumptions constitute stigma, a negative stereotype that involves labelling, othering, and discrimination. In addition to causing psychological harm and social divisiveness, stigma has serious material consequences, with a "dramatic bearing on the distribution of life chances in such areas as earnings, housing, criminal involvement, [and] health" (Link and Bruce 2001, 363).

The mothers and fathers who participated in this research encounter stigma all the time. There is, however, considerable variation in how they respond to it. Tyler lashes out. On one occasion, he threatened to "beat the crap" out of a newcomer to The 601 who had taken Tyler's laundry out of the washer and heaped it on the floor. "What the hell are you doing, man?" Tyler yelled, "Those are *my wife's* clothes!" The outreach coordinator hurried from her office but Kyle signalled that he would deal with it. He put an arm around Tyler, walked him outside, and listened supportively as he continued to blow off steam. Tyler's wife, Lisa, had suffered a miscarriage a few days before. He was on edge with grief and anger. "It was the worst thing that's happened in a long time," Tyler explained. He had found Lisa at home crying and in pain. Tyler's grief was a response to losing the baby that he and Lisa had wanted very badly. His anger, although targeted toward The 601 newcomer, was also a response to what he perceived to be the discriminatory care that Lisa had received at the hospital. "I [took] her to the emergency room, and they treated us like shit. Like, 'you got HIV and you're addicted, and it's the reason that your wife lost the baby.' They kept saying that." Kyle described it similarly, "Tyler told me that the hospital nurses kept zooming in on it, the drugs and booze and hepatitis C and HIV. Saying it's why Lisa got so sick and the baby died." Tyler and Lisa confirmed that she has HIV and HCV, but she had not used drugs (including alcohol) since learning she was pregnant. However, they had not been given the opportunity to explain that at the hospital.

These kinds of health care encounters – reported by 85 per cent of the research participants – reflect the power of stigma to offend and demoralize those confronted by it. In her study of pregnant and addicted women who live in daily rent hotels in the Mission district of San Francisco, Kelly Knight (2015, 53) finds that negative health care experiences lead many of the women to avoid or refuse medical care, including prenatal care, altogether. This can, of course, have serious and long-term consequences for both mothers and babies. There are similarly grave consequences for the PWAS at AIDS Saskatoon who are dissuaded from seeking health care. Arterial damage, injection site infection, abscesses, cotton fever, and respiratory arrest are only some of the effects of injection drug use if medical attention is not consistently sought. Untreated or sporadically treated HIV can result in serious infections (such as pneumonia, toxoplasmosis, and tuberculosis), neurological disorders (including the usually fatal condition known as multifocal leukoencephalopathy), and some types of cancer. When stigma keeps vulnerable patients from seeking the care they need, the results can be devastating not only for the patients but for the families who take care of them. "My boy has got HIV," Theresa explained. "He's a proud and good Cree man and doesn't like to be singled out as a no-good degenerate. The drug use, HIV, hepatitis C, it's all the people see and they treat him real bad. So he doesn't go to the doctor.... I cry and can't bear watching him suffer."

In addition to exemplifying the deterrent effects of stigma, the research participants' descriptions of discriminatory health care also illustrate the lack of differentiation between HIV and its related conditions. In the verbatim quotes cited above, clustered references to HIV, drug use, and other conditions are followed by the singular nominative pronoun "it": "The drug use, HIV, hepatitis C, *it*'s all the people see." This phrasing was used repeatedly by forty-four participants. In all cases, the discussion did not centre on any singular condition but on the effects of all the conditions combined. This phrasing represents more than conversational convenience. It represents the HIV syndemic.

As described in the introductory chapter, syndemics are interactions among health conditions that increase the burden of illness beyond comorbidity (Singer and Clair 2003). The synergistic relationship among HIV, addiction, and related conditions such as poverty, HCV, and tuberculosis, however, do not only manifest clinically. Syndemics are shaped and experienced culturally through common understandings of everyday experiences, through prevailing social stigma, and through the stories that those affected tell.

The research participants define and respond to the health challenges they face in an integrated way. One condition folds into the others, as do the treatments. Although the HIV syndemic is now well recognized in clinical settings, the unique syndemic logic employed by those living with HIV is often a source of frustration for practitioners. Lisa explained, "At the hospital, the nurse got mad at me when she asked if I was still in treatment and I said yes. She comes back later and [says], 'No, you haven't been in the methadone program for six months.' She rolled her eyes, all bitchy like, like I'm dumb or something. But I was talking about treatment for hep C and HIV. I was talking about the whole ball of wax. Maybe *she's* the dumb one."

On several occasions, I had the opportunity to discuss this research with a friend who is a public health nurse. She offered a different take. "A lot of times, there is frustration with what health care providers see as a lack of specificity or precision in the accounts of HIV patients," she explained. "A question about HIV treatment will be answered with rambling stories about addictions counselling. A question about compliance with the methadone program will be met with stories about being evicted from an apartment. It can be really hard to get accurate information. This becomes especially frustrating when we need information about a child and we have no one other than the mother to consult."

From an anthropological perspective, the issue here is not necessarily the accuracy of the information provided by HIV patients. The issue is that the cultural logic that patients use to define their conditions and treatments in far-reaching and integrated ways is considerably different from the reductionist and biomedical logic employed by most health care providers. Whereas biomedical understandings of disease rest on the separation and isolation of pathogens and symptoms, cultural understandings of disease rest on interconnections and context. Communicating across the gulf that separates these two logics is, at best, difficult. At worst, miscommunication between health care providers and patients results in the marginalization and stigmatization of those already vexed and rendered vulnerable by HIV. Cyndy Baskin and Bela McPherson (2014) identify the problem as a lack of reciprocal learning. Mothers and fathers who are marginalized by cultural heritage, HIV, addictions, poverty, and the like are expected to learn what health care providers and social service workers want from them. There is little effort made to learn what priorities the PWAS may have for themselves and their families. The result is an escalation of resentment and suspicion among those who are in need of health care and social service support.

The stigma associated with the HIV syndemic is part of the overall burden of illness that AIDS Saskatoon mothers and fathers carry. Their responses to it involve significant parental cooperation and coordination. The research participants do not separate the stigma they face into that which targets addiction versus that which targets HIV or any other related condition. The stigma is seen to be far-reaching, entangling almost every aspect of their lives. It is this all-encompassing stigma that the research participants identify as a particular threat to their children. Most commonly, AIDS Saskatoon mothers and fathers work to protect their children by sheltering them from parental drug use itself. "The best way to keep the kids safe from the haters is to keep the drugs away from them," Dennis explained. "Sure, I still used [drugs] when I was raising Jordy up. But he never saw it. When he heard people talk crap about me, he could walk away because the words didn't mean nothing because he never saw me doing nothing." Sally similarly noted that she never used drugs around her children, and Thomas attested to it: "The kids don't see us do drugs. We are *real* careful about that. And we're *real* careful to make sure that the family are around the kids when we're sick 'cause of the hepatitis treatments. That way, [the kids] don't miss out on nothing while we're getting high or getting treatment. We don't want nobody to hold nothing against the kids."

In just over 70 per cent of the interviews, references to sheltering children from parental drug use were coupled with references to the importance of educating children about the harsh realities of the HIV syndemic. For example, Janice explained:

> I've been on my own since sixteen, since I run from the last foster place. I don't have money. Yeah, I use [drugs]. But I know how to take care of my girls. The most important thing I do is keep them safe from the street. I don't use [drugs] when they're around. I keep them safe by sending them off with [their father's] family. Me and him teach them about HIV and the ART drugs and why we're sick. And teach them how to stand up strong to the haters who talk shit about us, the people who think that because they got more than us and their health is not as bad that they're better than us. I know one thing for sure, they don't have more love to give.

As part of the photovoice component of this research, Nancy – a twenty-two-year-old woman who worked in the sex trade to support her two brothers and mother, and who frequently cared for her nieces and nephews – took five pictures of the drug paraphernalia that she routinely used. She described, in great detail, the considerable lengths to which she and her boyfriend would go to ensure that the children in her care had no access to anything drug related. "Both [my boyfriend] and me are, like, totally honest with the kids about the drugs, the hep, the HIV, all of it," Nancy asserted. "No sugar-dipping life. But the drug stuff stays totally locked away. We use [the drugs] in the storage closet, *never* where the kids can get at us." I followed by asking why it is important not to "sugar dip" descriptions of addiction and HIV. She replied without hesitation, "Because sugar won't protect them from the shit that the other kids, the neighbours, the teachers, and the doctors are going to throw at them. Me and [my boyfriend] are ... on the same page with the whole family about this." Nancy continued by drawing the common analogy between the buffalo as a pre-colonial source of survival for the Cree and Sioux Peoples of the plains, and education as the key cultural source today: "Education is the new buffalo. They say that at [the youth centre]. We got to work together to make sure the kids know what they got to know so that the shit that gets said to them won't hurt."

Protecting and educating children is part of what Doug referred to earlier as the work of love. "The work of love?" Kyle was amused.

He repeated the phrase with great animation. He turned to Doug and blew him a kiss. "Did I really say that?" Doug asked. "You sure did," Rachel interjected. "I was sitting right here and Pam got it on her recorder." Doug laughed, "Well hell, I guess I'm a softie!" Kyle continued his good-natured teasing, and Doug jokingly returned the barbs: "This from a guy who sucks up all the time with his '*Thiiis* would be *interestiiiiing.*'"

In most social research, participant interviews are kept completely confidential. Many of the interviews conducted in this research adhered to this tradition. However, there is often more openness and comradery among research participants in anthropological fieldwork. This was certainly case in The 601. Participants sought out other PWAS to discuss matters that had come up in the interviews. They talked openly about who was on the "interview list" and frequently wanted others to sit in on their interviews to confirm and affirm experiences. They worked together to take notes and clip newspaper articles that they thought would be relevant. Throughout the research, there was a participatory engagement with the topic that allowed collective as well as individual perspectives to be shared. It became increasingly clear that in the context of HIV, talking about parenting, like parenting itself, involves a family spirit among the PWAS at AIDS Saskatoon. Within the broader kin-based system of child care, the cooperation between mothers and fathers is most apparent as they attempt to protect children from the painful stigma that is associated with the HIV syndemic.

The mothers and fathers who participated in this research also work together when they feel pressured to conform to a nuclear family structure. Dennis explained that the consequences of not appearing as an intact nuclear family are as well known as they are confusing. "Look at what happened to Isabel," he said. "They took Mark away because the [CFS workers] wanted only a mom and dad, not a full family. Huh? Why isn't a full family better?" Doug expressed concern that his extended family is "too Native and too rez" to be seen as "normal" in the urban environment of Saskatoon. He therefore worked with his wife "to make up appearances," saying, "My wife and me, we take the kids to the doctor and go to teacher meetings together, stuff like that. [My wife] *should* be taking the kids' aunties. They're the ones that know more about when kids are sick ... and way more about school stuff. But I go, sit beside [my wife] to make up appearances.... Just like the bubble people, them fancy White folks who live in a bubble."

In most public and private sectors, there is an institutional bias in favour of the racially privileged, financially secure, and heterosexual two-parent family. In the criminal justice system, "familial ideology explains disparities in sentencing for similar offences; female offenders who have 'normal families' and assume appropriate gender roles receive more lenient sentencing" (Boyd 1999, 18). In health care, a nuclear family structure is associated with having fewer unmet health-related needs as well as a better quality of care and support (Bramlett and Blumberg 2007). Dorothy Smith (1993) argues that ideological codes for families are much like genetic codes. They reproduce characteristic forms and orders. These codes define what is "normal," and broken codes are believed (often erroneously) to produce abnormalities and deficiencies.

The appearance of conformity with the nuclear family code takes work, and sometimes deceit. "Even after we broke up, I used to use [my ex-husband's] address," Rachel explained. "He'd lie and say I lived there even after I moved out. We didn't want nobody thinking that we weren't like the White families." Minimizing the extent of their poverty, denying ongoing drug use, de-emphasizing extended family's involvement in child care, and overemphasizing intensive parenting are some of ways in which mothers and fathers work together to emulate the codified nuclear family. There is frequently a risk involved with such deceit. Services may be denied; surveillance may increase. However, AIDS Saskatoon mothers and fathers generally assign an even greater risk to having their families deemed deficient. Of course, judgments of familial deficiency, like judgments of parental deficiency, are far-reaching and encountered outside the HIV/AIDS realm as well. But judgment is not equally assigned across cultural and racialized contexts. The research participants are well aware that racially privileged and affluent families affected by addictions (HIV as well, but particularly addictions) are more likely to be spared the harsh stigma that the PWAS at AIDS Saskatoon face. "I drink beer and smoke crack," Rachel said. "Rich White girls drink expensive wine and take little pills. We both love our kids but their love counts for more because they're rich, and White. I want my love to count, too."

In her autoethnography of the Upper East Side, Manhattan, Wednesday Martin (2015, 186–7) confirms Rachel's characterization:

> The mommies I knew drank – white wine, vodka, tequila, and, for those bent on male approval or setting themselves apart, scotch or some other "guy" whiskey – every night.... For many of the women with kids I knew in Manhattan – women who wore sunglasses on Wednesday and Thursday and Friday mornings – drinking was a way to self-soothe and self-medicate, a solution of sorts, something to bring on sleep, a reward for surviving the cab ride, the crosstown schlep, the argument with the nanny.... What struck me as I drank with the women around me was that, be it psychological, social or emotional, the drinking was mainly, to my eye, tribal. It is virtually *comme il faut*.... [It] is part of the culture.

Among Upper East Side mothers – who live in a neighbourhood that routinely ranks first on Forbes's "priciest zip code" list, where median home prices exceed US$6.5 million, and where private nursery schools have annual tuitions of US$40,000 – benzodiazepines are "a girl's best friend." Ativan, Xanax, Valium, Ambien, and Klonopin are among the drugs that are used with great frequency, often in combination with alcohol (Martin 2015, 187). Drug use is woven into the cultural fabric of Park Avenue mothers and families. Yet Martin's ethnography contains no mention of state surveillance and lost custody, nor does it contain descriptions of "abusive junkies." There are definitely other types of judgment that Park Avenue mothers make about each other, but the kind of surveillance and stigma that poor mothers and families face in the highly racialized and marginalized contexts of HIV/AIDS in Saskatchewan are absent.

In Canada, the rates of "risky drinking" (consuming more than two drinks per day) among women increased from 44 per cent in 2007 to 56 per cent in 2013 (PHAC 2016, 9). Binge drinking (consuming five or more drinks on any one occasion) among women across North America has increased at a rate seven times that of men. Women in university and those with well-paying, professional jobs account for much of this increase (Bulloch et al. 2016). Similarly, professional women in Canadian urban centres are among the most likely to be over-prescribed benzodiazepines (Currie 2004; Herie and Skinner

2010), and rates of benzodiazepine use have increased by 13 per cent since 2007 (Posadzki 2013). When it comes to the opioid crisis in the country, Carly Weeks and Karen Howlett (2016) argue that recreational drug use accounts for only part of the profile. In 2015, doctors in Canada were writing one opioid prescription for every two Canadians (Dyck 2017), including White, educated, and middle-class professionals. Although the number of overall opioid prescriptions has decreased by roughly 2 per cent in last five years (Canadian Institutes for Health Research 2019), Canada remains one of the largest per capita consumer of these drugs.

There is some state surveillance and monitoring of drug use in all communities. However, that which exists in marginalized and poor communities is far more intense than in affluent ones. To try to evade this surveillance and seek out the protections granted to those with race and class privilege, AIDS Saskatoon mothers and fathers work together to create a nuclear family veneer. Their families, as discussed previously, actually extend across communities and child care is often undertaken collectively. However, the research participants represent their families differently when they feel pressured by health care workers, teachers, child service workers, or criminal justice workers to do so. This is a clear point of articulation between mothering and fathering, one that allows the research participants to further protect themselves and their families from HIV-related stigma.

CONCLUSION

Between 1991 and 2007, the National Institute of Child and Human Development in the United States undertook a longitudinal study that explored the links among home environments, child characteristics, and child care situations in over thirteen hundred families. There are many important insights about American family life to be learned from this research. However, Joan Wolf (2016) persuasively argues that the study is so centred on maternal attributes and behaviours – what anthropologists would identify as matricentricism – that fathers are rarely considered. For example, in exploring the effect of parents' intelligence on how care environments shape children's cognitive development, the researchers rely only on measures of mothers' education, verbal intelligence, and vocabulary. Indicators specific to fathers are not considered even though conclusions about *parental* intelligence are drawn (631). The roles that fathers and other caregivers play in child care are minimized or overlooked altogether. "Researchers," Wolf argues, "can find significance only where they look for it, and when their gaze is fixed on maternal variables, they cannot separate the dynamics in question ... from the caretaker engaged in them" (634).

On that busy afternoon in The 601, Dennis, Doug, Tyler, and Kyle ensured that this study of mothering in the context of Saskatchewan's HIV epidemic would not exclude fathers and fathering. Although the initial focus of the research remained strong, the opportunity to explore how mothers and fathers work together and within a wider network of kin-care to nurture their children and to honour their families provided invaluable insight. In some ways, motherhood and fatherhood figure into the research participants' lives as separate but complementary realms. Drawing on their own experiences with the criminal justice system, fathers take on the task of teaching and guiding children to avoid conflict with the law. It is, as Doug and others claimed, a father's job. There are, however, two sites of tight connection between mothering and fathering: protecting children from the stigma associated with the HIV syndemic and enacting a nuclear family structure in order to seek out the safeguards from the stigma that those in privileged communities appear to enjoy. This creates a continuum of parental connectedness, from the uniquely paternal task of breaking the pattern of intergenerational incarceration to the coordinated efforts to protect children and families from discriminatory judgment. AIDS Saskatoon mothers and fathers move back and forth along this continuum, rendering the contours of maternal and paternal care ever clearer as they go.

The experiences of Indigenous men are critical to understanding how fatherhood and fathering fits into the profile of HIV-affected parenting. Jessica Ball (2010, 125) argues that because Indigenous fatherhood is not as culturally storied as Indigenous motherhood, and because the legacy of colonial policies of Indigenous displacement remains strong, "when Indigenous men become fathers, most are venturing into a role that has no personal resonance." Moreover, given that there is so little research that focuses on, or social advocacy for,

Indigenous fathers, they may be "the most socially excluded population in North America" (126). The perspectives, priorities, and paternal dedication of the twenty Indigenous men who participated in this research, therefore, not only contribute to our understanding of the Indigenized terrain of HIV in Saskatchewan, they also contribute to the cultural history of First Nations and Métis fatherhood that is only beginning to be told. This is a history that Kyle understood to be particularly important to the younger Indigenous fathers in The 601. "Dennis and me, we're two of the oldest guys here," he said. "We want the younger guys to know that even if they're [drug] users, even with the HIV and hep and even being poor and maybe being homeless, even with all that, they can be good fathers, good men.... There's a place for them there. I hope there's somebody to tell them that after Dennis and me aren't around."

Dennis died on an unseasonably warm November night. He was writing a letter to his daughter when his heart abruptly stopped. His son Jordan found him the next morning. Dennis was well loved in The 601. When his heart stopped, our hearts broke. A year and a half later, on a brilliant June morning, Kyle died. He had developed lung cancer and it had progressed rapidly. When I visited him in the hospital, we chatted for a while. I described some new research ideas in the hopes that he would say, "That would be interesting" just one more time. But he didn't. He was too tired. At his memorial service, a staff member at AIDS Saskatoon offered a beautiful eulogy. She imagined Dennis and Kyle, long-time and fiercely loyal friends, reunited in the world beyond us, free from pain, and dancing in the northern lights. As she spoke, Doug held his teenaged daughter in his arms, and they both wept.

5

Loss

> Like molasses, grief is thick, slow-moving, and sneaky, coating every surface it touches and affecting everything that lies within and between it.
>
> – *Rhaisa Williams (2016, 18)*

Rachel is a talented tattoo artist. Because she is both HIV- and HCV-positive, Rachel does not get her tattoos at a commercial parlour. She uses her own ink and needles to create beautiful designs on her forearms, hands, ankles, and feet. "But, doesn't it *hurt*?" My question betrayed my ignorance not only about tattoos (of course it hurts) but also about Rachel's ability to withstand pain. "She's the toughest tough guy out there," Doug exclaimed with brotherly pride. "Her spirit is steel." Rachel's steel cracked when her two sons were removed from her care. We had been talking about the important place that her children hold in her life when she stopped midsentence and started to cry. "When you lose your kids, the sky goes dark. Like the worst storm in the world is coming," she managed to say through tears. "It don't matter how much you love your kids, if you got HIV, you'll lose your kids, and the sky goes dark."

Rachel's oldest son was being assessed for learning disabilities and Rachel had missed two appointments in a row. School officials had notified CFS. Rachel explained that "the [caseworker] didn't let me say nothing, to tell her why I missed the appointments. She said she needed to do a 'risk assessment.' I didn't know what that was and I knew that there wasn't no point in asking because she would just bullshit me and not let me talk.... So I punched her." Rachel's sons were then deemed to be at risk for physical abuse and placed in temporary foster care. The police investigated the CFS caseworker's claim that Rachel had assaulted her. No charges were laid but Rachel was warned that they "would be watching." Rachel therefore blamed herself when Doug was arrested for drug possession several days later: "Them cops wouldn't have been around except for they was watching me like they said and they knew that we was using. Now my brother is probably gonna go to jail."

Francine, a sixty-year-old mother of four, heard Rachel crying and joined us. "You know what this is like?" Francine asked. "It's like *mescinewin*." She continued:

> Rachel, Isabel, Sally, and me were at [the Indian and Métis Friendship Centre] when [a Cree Elder] was there and was talking to us about *mescinewin*. He explained that it means losing your whole family to a disease. I never heard that before.... It means that a disease takes your whole family. That's what happened with smallpox. That's what happened when families went off to TB hospitals. That's what happens when alcoholism kills off your whole family. And it's happening now. HIV, hepatitis C, drugs, it's like TB and polio was when I was young.... You can be the toughest bird in the tree, but if *mescinewin* comes, you lose your family, you lose everything.

Francine and her brother had bulbospinal polio as children. Her brother had died. The poliovirus had paralyzed his diaphragm, and his young body, having just endured tuberculosis, could not withstand another infection. Although Francine survived, the paralytic disease took away her ability to walk. She relied on crutches for the rest of her life. The crutches gave her some mobility, but they were also used against her in residential school. "Teachers would take them away from me when they heard me speaking Cree, and I would have to crawl across the floor, pulling myself with my arms.... The teachers, they goaded the kids into calling me names. They called me...."

Francine paused and Rachel interjected, "a snake? They called you a snake." We sat in silence for a long time. Rachel and Francine looked at each other, nodding in silent understanding of each other's circumstances. *Mescinewin* took on a highly emotional meaning in this exchange. The HIV syndemic, like the polio epidemic some fifty years before, involved losing children, losing brothers, losing dignity.

A few days later, Michaela and I were in the upstairs lounge at AIDS Saskatoon. "Rachel and Fran told me about the *mescinewin* stuff that you guys talked about," she began. "It sure makes sense to me. I mean, I'm not Aboriginal, obviously. But losing your family 'cause of a disease is on my mind a lot." Two years earlier, Michaela had surgery on her spine. Injection drug use and HIV can be predisposing conditions for serious spinal infections. "They had to put screws into the bones in my neck because I had a real bad staph infection in my back bone," she explained. It was a terrifying time in her life:

> I kept thinking how much I love my daughter. I love everything about her. But if I die, then she loses the only person she has. Nobody can count on her dad for much. We have our people in The 601, but that's it. Like, she was only seven and I almost passed away. What would have happened to her?... It's terrifying to think about.... The pain after my surgery was so bad. I had to work to pay the rent and buy food. It was really physical work in the meat plant, and it was so painful. So, I started doing ecstasy so I could stand it. I almost died again when I [overdosed].... And what would have happened to [my daughter]? She would have lost everything.... It's like the way Fran talked about *mescinewin*.

In terms of the frequency with which a topic was discussed as well as the extent of narrative elaboration, loss was the most common and prominent theme that emerged in interviews. Every interview included at least two detailed discussions of loss and several more indirect references to it. Loss was also a common theme, second to conflict with the law, in the interviews conducted with AIDS Saskatoon fathers. In all interviews, loss was discussed primarily in relation to child apprehension. Other losses figured into our discussions as well – the death of a family member, miscarriage, the imagined loss that others would endure after a participant's death – but the primary focus was child apprehension. This is not surprising given that, in the early 2000s, three times more Indigenous children and youth were in state care across Canada than during the height of the residential school system in the 1940s (Cull 2006, 144). This is a reality faced by both Indigenous and non-Indigenous research participants who live in an environment where child apprehension is an ongoing threat. The experiences of loss among the non-Indigenous participants are framed by a different political history, but they unfold in the same cultural space as those of the Indigenous participants.

In the years since the fieldwork of this project was completed, I have presented the findings related to loss to various academic and health care audiences. After most presentations, I am asked how love figures into the picture: "Do the participants ever talk about loving, or even caring for, their children, or is it entirely about loss?" Mothers draw particular attention, as many questioners follow up by asking how I can know *"for sure"* that the women love their children. Researchers who work with mothers with cancer, malnutrition, tuberculosis, or malaria rarely, if ever, receive similar questions. Audiences appear to accept without question that mothers with those conditions love their children. The maternal love expressed and experienced by drug-using and HIV-affected mothers is not similarly assumed or accepted. However, love did indeed emerge as a prominent theme in all components of the research. Importantly, though, almost 70 per cent of the references to love were embedded in discussions of loss. Another 10 per cent of the references to love served as a prologue to discussions of potential or anticipated loss, such as when Michaela contemplated what her possible death would have meant for her well-loved daughter. Therefore, engaging ethnographically with maternal love amidst the HIV syndemic in Saskatchewan involves navigating the stormy sites of loss. This chapter traces that navigation by first considering how emotions are culturally grounded and then exploring the three dimensions of loss – deprivation, deficiency, and privation.

"THE WRONG KIND OF UPSET": THE ANTHROPOLOGY OF EMOTION

In their formative review article on the anthropology of emotion, Catherine Lutz and Geoffrey White (1986, 431) argue that "incorporating emotion into ethnography ... entails presenting a fuller view of *what is at stake* for people in everyday life.... At issue is not only the humanity of our images but the adequacy of our understanding of cultural and social forms." In the prestigious Malinowski Memorial Lecture at the London School of Economics almost thirty years later, Andrew Beatty (2014, 560) reaffirms the importance of engaging emotion in our work: "Whether we think in pictures or stories, ... speak as *we* or *I*, love or loathe anecdotes, we are all narrators because we all have emotions; and emotions [demand] their own story."

There is no cross-cultural category of emotion. There are feelings, thoughts, sentiments, and responses, "but only in Western thought," Beatty (2014, 559) argues, "do they cohere in the package we call emotion. Most languages lack a superordinate emotion category." This leads to considerable tension among scholars across the social and biological sciences. There are disagreements between those who believe emotion to be primarily a biological and evolutionary phenomenon and those who believe it to be volitional and cultural. There are those who emphasize the universality of emotion, as Paul Ekman (2007) does in his study of how readily people from different cultural backgrounds recognize emotions represented by facial expressions. In contrast, there are those who emphasize the cultural particularity of emotion, as Catherine Lutz (1998) does in her work among the Ifaluk people of Micronesia. Lutz demonstrates that the Ifaluk emotion of *fago* is a unique composite of compassion, love, and sadness. It has no direct corollary in any other cultural context. Theories about the universal essence of sadness or love, therefore, do not fully capture the emotional experience of *fago*.

The debates rage on. Among researchers who otherwise agree that basic emotions are experienced in the same way across all cultures, there is dispute over how basic is basic. To what extent is there "room for cultural fine-tuning" within broad categories of fear, anger, happiness, and sadness (Anderson 2011, 319)? Anthropologists and social psychologists often agree that there are cultural bases of emotion, but we argue over how we can best account for inter-group differences in emotional expression within the same cultural context. Is emotion more idiosyncratic or collective? Moreover, to what extent is emotion inextricable from human communication? Philosopher Martha Nussbaum (2001, 149) argues that language can change the very nature of an emotion. But if a language contains no term for a particular emotion – for example, according to linguist Anna Wierzbicka (2004, 581), Polish does not include a term equivalent to "grief" – is that experience lacking in the lives of native speakers?

Fortunately, the scholarly tensions that arise within the anthropology of emotion tend to be productive ones. Most anthropologists now understand emotion in more holistic and robust ways than those who remain tethered to one approach. Glen Shepard's (2002) analysis of grief among the Matsigenka people of the Peruvian Amazon, for instance, strikes a balance. Matsigenka expressions of grief include withdrawal from social contact, loss of appetite, immune system depression, and the sense that something bad has happened. This is a response found not only across human cultures but in many animal species as well. Yet among the Matsigenka, long-term feelings of confusion and despair are uniquely ascribed to the dead, not to bereaved mourners. Those who express grief beyond the three days allotted for mourning are considered pathological. This, in turn, fundamentally affects how grief is actually experienced, making it highly specific to the Matsigenka cultural context. In Shepard's ethnography (and others like it), emotion is represented as simultaneously universal, culturally specific, and individual. As Andrew Beatty (2014, 557) states, "No account of emotions ... could justly privilege one [facet] over another. Take away one dimension and the whole thing collapses."

The majority of non-ethnographic research on emotion and HIV does not engage with the scholarly debates described above. Instead, it rests on an assumption that emotions are experienced the same way by HIV patients everywhere, regardless of cultural context. This assumption is largely the result of homogenizing methodologies. Researchers rely heavily on psychological instruments that rarely accommodate the influence of culture. In a study of the social sharing of emotions among HIV patients in the Dominican Republic, Cantisano et al. (2015) relied exclusively on the Quality of Sharing Inventory (QSI), a questionnaire developed by another team of researchers in Greece to explore how social interaction helps alleviate pre-operative stress in patients undergoing cardiac surgery (Panagopoulou et al. 2006). The QSI is derived from interviews with ten patients in a Greek city hospital and ten healthy adults who were asked about the circumstances under which talking to another person made them feel better or worse. Cantisano and colleagues assume that the optimal circumstances for talking about HIV-related emotional experiences transcend the national, cultural, and linguistic differences between Greece and the Dominican Republic, not to mention the differences between clinical conditions. Anthropologists reject this inattention to local cultural context.

I met with Rachel for our third interview several weeks after her sons were removed from her care. She had taken notes from her follow-up appointment with Social Services and asked if we could go through them. One of the caseworker's statements included the observation that Rachel had supposedly shown "no signs of distress" when her sons were taken from her home. Rachel was particularly upset by this comment. "*Yesss*, I was real freaked out," she explained. "But I know better than to show weakness. Those [caseworkers] smell weakness and go in for the kill. Plus, she was pissing me off so bad. All my energies was going to not punching her. Don't I get points for not knocking her out?" The sorrow Rachel previously shared with Francine had given way to anger directed toward the caseworker and the perceived injustice of the situation.

Rachel is among twenty-one mothers who, through the course of this research, expressed frustration that their emotional states are mischaracterized during their encounters with service providers. Theresa's concern over son Caleb's drug use and HIV is repeatedly misinterpreted by a correctional service worker. "Caleb's probation officer told me once that he could tell I had 'issues' because I don't cry enough," she said. "He said he sees that I don't care about Cale 'cause I don't show no emotion. It hurt so much to hear him say that. I started to cry. Then the [probation officer] goes, 'Nice crocodile tears'.... I had to look up what it means. I swear, I wasn't crying crocodile tears." Eileen, a forty-two-year-old Cree mother of two adult children, shared a similar experience by recalling when her son was in his late teens:

> We were living in [another city] and my son had started to sell his Ritalin to some of the neighbourhood guys. But I didn't know that then. My son and me were in the living room colouring little pictures with my daughter who was, like, six or seven then. I look out the window and I see the mobile crisis van pull up. They come storming in saying, "We got reports that you're using [drugs] in here".... I roll up my sleeves so they can see my arms and say, "Look, I'm clean. I'm taking my HIV meds. I'm healthy. We're doing good."

> My son gets real mad at them, but I just stay real calm. One of them says, "This is serious." He goes, "Me? An outreach worker comes into my house, thinking I'm not taking care of my kid, I'd be upset. You're not upset." I didn't say nothing. But how could they tell if I was upset?... Social workers should have sympathy, not come storming in and judging whether I'm the wrong kind of upset.

Much of the misreading of the research participants' emotions is tied to the long legacy of colonial and Eurocentric misrepresentations of Indigenous Peoples. Distorted depictions of an Indigenous "flat affect" – absent or lacking emotions among those of First Nations and Métis heritage – fuel disparaging and racist assumptions that Indigenous cultures, and especially Indigenous mothers, are inferior (Ing 2006). Randi Cull (2006, 143), for example, details how Indigenous mothers were blamed for the high rates of tuberculosis on First Nations reserves in the late nineteenth and early twentieth centuries. Government reports from the time contain damning and racist depictions of emotionally withholding mothers in order to deny state culpability for the high rates of child mortality and to justify child apprehension. "The theme that links the state's past and present treatment of Aboriginal mothers," Cull (2006, 141) argues, is "the implicit notion that Aboriginal women are 'unfit' parents." The ongoing misinterpretation of maternal emotions helps to fuel this notion. However, almost one hundred years of research and first-hand testimony demonstrate that Indigenous emotional repertoires are strong and varied even though overt emotionalism may not be culturally emphasized (LaFramboise, Trimble, and Mohatt 1990; Waldram 2004). Emotional equanimity is often more highly valued in Indigenous communities, particularly in the context of Indigenous-settler relations where power inequities are acute (Waldram 1997).

The women who participated in this research are frustrated that their calm reactions are misconstrued. They are also fearful that showing any feelings of despair will exacerbate accusations that they are inadequate mothers. "Imagine if I started hollering ... the day they stormed in to my apartment?" Eileen pondered. "They would have said right off that I was a wild Indian, an out-of-control junkie whose meds are making her cuckoo crazy. For sure, they would have said that." Theresa's experience with Caleb's probation officer confirms much of Eileen's characterization: "The next time me and Caleb meet with the guy, he starts sniping at

Caleb so I try to stand up for him. My voice gets tight, like I'm gonna cry. Then [the officer] tells me to leave, says I'm 'irrational' and 'moody' and says 'maybe it's your AIDS meds.' *What?* So, first I'm not upset enough, then my voice shakes so he thinks I'm 'irrational.' I mean, *what*?"

In these no-win situations, AIDS Saskatoon mothers are afraid that any emotional reaction will be misread by those in power. They therefore try to minimize their responses. Rachel recalled making a conscious effort to sit motionless as her sons left with the caseworker. She did not want to compound the loss that she knew was coming, saying, "If I showed any feelings, they'd be used against me. The boys might get taken away forever. They might not make it in the world without us, without ever seeing the rez again. So I sat there, breathing in and breathing out, not wanting to show nothing. Not showing how mad or scared I was. Not crying. Not fighting. Not screaming for help. Not running. All those things were inside me when [the caseworker] skipped out with my boys. But I couldn't dare let none of it show."

It is impossible to disentangle the anger, fear, and sadness that Rachel felt that afternoon. It is possible, however, to identify distinct dimensions of the research participants' experiences of loss and explore the emotional expressions of them.

GRIEF: DEPRIVATION, DEFICIENCY, AND PRIVATION

Grief is a response to loss. It can involve shock, sadness, fear, anger, guilt, despair, loneliness, and much more. There is a common saying in Britain: "Grief for the dead is a pain that proves we are human." Yet grief is neither the sole province of humans nor of death. The Seaworld polar bear Szenja died from grief in April 2017 when she was separated from her friend Snowflake, with whom she shared an enclosure for twenty years. Ecologist Marc Bekoff (2011) explains that chimpanzees mourn when they are separated from troop mates. Elephants cry when family members are captured. Service and pet dogs grieve the loss of their human as well as canine companions. However, variation in the expression of grief is greatest among humans, and that fact is largely attributable to culture. Psychologist Paul Rosenblatt (2008, 207) argues that "culture creates, influences, shapes, limits, and defines grieving, sometimes profoundly. Understanding the complex entanglement between culture and grieving is a first step towards theorizing about grief in a culturally attuned way."

Few scholars have contributed as meaningfully to the scholarship on the cultural dimensions of maternal grief as anthropologist Nancy Scheper-Hughes. In her work in Alto de Cruzeiro, a poor *favela* (slum) in northern Brazil where rates of infant and child mortality are among the highest in the world, Scheper-Hughes explores mothers' responses to their children's suffering and death. She argues that Alto de Cruzeiro culture is organized "to defend women against the psychological ravagings of grief" (Scheper-Hughes 1993, 430). Women are cajoled, counselled, and supported to be emotionally detached from their ailing and dying children, and to shed no tears at their deaths. Showing outward signs of grief is seen as emotional excess and is viewed as both individually and collectively unhealthy. "The question remains," Scheper-Hughes posits, "whether the dry-eyed stoicism and nonchalant air of Alto mothers are merely 'superficial' and skin-deep, covering up a 'depth of sorrow, loss and longing'" (430). She concludes that the emotional distance that Alto mothers are able to keep from grief is very real.

In the AIDS Saskatoon research, I found the opposite. The women who participated in this research experience profound grief when their children are removed from their care. Their grief involves a sense of deprivation and deficiency. For some, grief also involves a largely inexpressible and private sense of dismemberment. Although the research participants go to great lengths to remain as emotionally calm as possible, they describe emotional "storms" as the child apprehension process unfolds. Among the twenty-five women who experienced or witnessed the removal of children from their homes or the homes of family members, twenty used metaphors of natural disasters to recount their loss. References to blizzards, wild fires, floods, earthquakes, mudslides, thunderstorms, tornados, hurricanes, and tsunamis appear over 120 times throughout the interviews. Like the mothers with whom Scheper-Hughes worked, AIDS Saskatoon mothers view the life-altering experience of child loss as a force of nature beyond their control. Unlike the mothers of Alto de Cruzeiro, however, the women who participated in this research are identified by social service workers, health care practitioners, and others as being culpable for their loss. This affects how the research participants express and experience grief.

Deprivation is the first and most immediate dimension that emerged in the research participants' narratives of loss. AIDS Saskatoon mothers express a clear sense that their lives and those of their children are extremely deprived by child apprehension. "I never had a lot of money," Janice explained, "but I never felt poor either. Most Aboriginal people don't got money but we're rich in lots of other ways. But then my kids got taken away after my HIV test came back positive. Then my girls and me learned what being poor was all about." Before her three youngest children were placed in the care of her twenty-two-year-old daughter, Anne feared that they would "disappear into the system." She recalled feeling "like a blizzard was gonna blow my house down. Like I could see it coming and I knew that it was gonna hit and my kids and I would lose everything.... I was so afraid because my kids' lives would be wrecked." Holding her hand up as if to indicate a high level and then letting it drop, she added, "It's like our lives would go from being a family, being together up here, to being low, having everything taken away. I was so scared." Charlotte, a twenty-eight-year-old Cree woman from Manitoba, described feeling as if she was being "robbed" when CFS was investigating allegations that she was neglecting her son: "It was like something was being taken away from us.... Like they were taking a little bit of our home every time they left. I don't think I've ever been so mad in my life. Why would they threaten to rob us like that, to take us away from each other? 'Cause I got hep C? That's crazy."

Anger and fear commonly accompany this sense of deprivation. The mothers who participated in this research experience these emotions in rapid and alternating succession. As Rachel recalled her first meeting with the caseworker, fear quickened to anger and then back to fear:

> I got so scared when she said she was going to do a "risk assessment" 'cause I missed my son's appointment. I thought, "You're taking my boys? What will happen to them?" I couldn't breathe. Then she wouldn't listen to nothing I said. I missed the call about [my son's] appointment because I left my phone at work. But she wouldn't listen. Then I got red-hot mad. I, you know, I hit her. Then, holy shit, I wanted to run. Grab my boys and run for our lives. I was so scared. I wanted to hide. Then I just started yelling

> at her, "You f'ing bitch," I was red-hot mad. I was going to lose my boys. I don't scare easy but I was so damn scared.

For the next fifteen minutes of the interview, Rachel alternated between descriptions of fear and of anger, the impulse to run and the urge to lash out. Anger and fear are usually acute emotional reactions. For Rachel and the majority of research participants, however, they are also longer-term responses, extending throughout and beyond the period of parental assessment.

In Saskatchewan, there are six circumstances that constitute grounds for risk assessment and child apprehension: physical abuse, sexual abuse and exploitation, physical neglect, emotional maltreatment, exposure to domestic violence or severe domestic disharmony, and failure to provide essential medical treatment. The vast majority of investigations into the safety and well-being of the research participants' children are in response to reports of suspected physical neglect or emotional maltreatment. As defined by The Child and Family Services Act (Government of Saskatchewan 2014, 5), physical neglect refers to acts of omission that entail "the failure to provide for the child's basic needs and appropriate level of care with respect to food, clothing, shelter, health/medical, hygiene, safety and supervision." Emotional maltreatment involves both emotional abuse and neglect, including excessive rejection, criticism, or demands, as well as the failure to provide adequate nurturance.

All caregivers must meet "minimum standards" of care as appropriate for a child's age and development. These standards, however, are not well defined, and there is considerable latitude in how they are interpreted. In 2000, the Supreme Court of Canada endorsed this latitude, ruling that CFS workers do not need a warrant to apprehend a child who they believe to be in potential danger. "This ruling," Randi Cull (2006, 150) points out, "opens the door for 'crystal ball' apprehensions; child welfare agents are provided the authority to 'predict' whether abuse 'might' occur." Many service providers are well trained to make judicious decisions. However, the latitude in predicting potential risk allows standards of individualistic motherhood and intensive mothering to be erroneously applied in cultural contexts where they are not the norm. This creates a significant and structural disadvantage for mothers who are already disadvantaged by the HIV syndemic.

AIDS Saskatoon mothers express intense anger toward this structural disadvantage. Janice has two daughters who were in foster care just outside her home reserve in central Saskatchewan. After successfully completing two parenting classes, adhering to the methadone treatment for addiction, and maintaining her ART for HIV as well as HCV, Janice gained back partial custody of her children. She spent weekends with her ten- and twelve-year-old daughters. Each Sunday night, she packed the girls' book bags for the start of the school week. "A couple of weeks ago," Janice recalled, "[the social worker] meets us when I drop the girls off at school on Monday morning, like she always does." She continued:

> [The social worker] sees that [my youngest daughter's] back pack is ripped a little, like [three centimetres]. She goes, "Why didn't you buy her a new one?" On the weekend, we were at the zoo with *kohkum* and my cousin so I didn't have time before the stores closed. Besides, I fixed it by putting duct tape on the inside. And besides, back packs cost a lot and I don't got much money. She tells me it's my responsibility to provide for my kids. And *then* she goes to [my daughter], "Do you feel bad about the things you don't have or your old clothes?" She said it *exactly* like that. So I says, "Holy shit, lady, my kids got everything they need. I don't got a lot of money but they got what they need." Then she goes, "Are you aware you just swore in front of your girls?" Then, I got told last week that I got to take another parenting class.... They're keeping my girls from me because of a ripped back pack? I'm getting punished for not having a lot of money.... I say bullshit to that.

In her study of parenthood among homeless youth, Deborah Connolly (2000, 284) argues that we must "question the equation that greater affluence equals greater love and a better life for a child." AIDS Saskatoon mothers similarly argue that their incomes and limited financial resources should not be a measure of their maternal competence or care. The physical toll of ART and methadone treatments restricts many of the research participants' abilities to work, and they face financial hardship and even poverty as a result. Their commitment to motherhood, however, remains strong. Janice explained that she can't work more than five retail shifts per week: "I'd be too tired to even lift my head to eat, never mind feed nobody else. The meds are too hard on me for me to work more than five shifts. But I *do* work. I *do* provide for the girls. And I *do* love them.... We got a whole family looking after them." She concluded our interview in tears, saying, "When [the social worker] called to say that she'd be 'more comfortable' if I took another class before I see my girls again, I felt, I don't know ... scared and frustrated and *mad*.... They keep taking [my daughters] away. It don't matter that I do everything that they tell me to do." The expected material requirements for child care appear to align with the affluence demanded by intensive mothering. Because of the structural inequities and health-related difficulties they face, AIDS Saskatoon mothers may never meet these requirements of affluence, leaving them with a strong sense of deprivation and unrelenting feelings of anger and fear.

Deficiency is the second dimension of loss that emerged throughout this research. Almost all of the women with whom I spoke called out the inadequacies in the social services that limit, mischaracterize, and threaten their relationships with their children. Research participants also recognize that others perceive them to be personally inadequate, to be mothers of lesser worth. "It don't matter that I got a job, love my kids, try every day to get my life on track," Rachel lamented. "All that people outside of The 601 see is a Native with HIV. And they sneer." Many AIDS Saskatoon mothers also internalize this assessment, expressing a deep sense of personal deficiency. When the crisis workers came into Eileen's home unannounced, for example, her effort to remain calm so as not to distress the children was interpreted as "the wrong kind of upset." This had a highly detrimental effect. "I felt like something was wrong with me," she recalled. "Maybe the HIV and hep C and the drug using, maybe it was making it so that my emotions weren't right. Like I was broken or cuckoo crazy. I felt like I wasn't good enough, even my upset wasn't good enough." Eileen had previously expressed concern that the social workers would draw this conclusion. Here, she internalizes the very characterization that she feared they would draw. Theresa similarly felt that she fell short of being "good enough" in all aspects of her life, including motherhood. "I don't cry enough for Caleb's probation officer, then he says I'm too moody," she recalled. "The doctors tell me to be patient, then they tell me I'm not working hard enough to get better. Caleb gets real pissed off with me, too. I'm around him too much, he says, then I'm never there when he needs me, he says. Maybe I'm just not good enough. I do the best I can, especially for Caleb, you know? I'm just, I don't know, just not enough.... When I'm dead, I probably won't be dead enough."

The research participants are not alone in feeling this way. The impossibly high standards set by models of individualistic motherhood cause many mothers, including affluent and healthy mothers, to feel inadequate. This sense of deficiency encompasses not only what mothers do but who they are. In recounting her experience as a first-time mother who, at eighteen years of age, was told she was "too young" and then as a second-time mother who, at thirty-six, was told she was "too old," Ariel Gore (2007, 758) explains that "the whole world tells us – in a thousand ways – that we are not enough for our children. The world tells us that we are ... too poor, too extravagant, too permissive, too controlling, too urban, too rural, too eccentric, too square, and everything in between." AIDS Saskatoon mothers receive these messages with great frequency and intensity. They therefore share a sense of deficiency with mothers in vastly different cultural contexts. The research participants also experience their perceived deficiency in ways particular to the chronicity, stigma, and Indigenization of HIV and addiction. This particular environment is cultivated, in part, through public sentiment, institutional practices, *and* social policy.

HIV/AIDS and addiction are currently represented in public health policy as chronic health conditions, not moral failings. Relapse and convalescence are cyclical components in the pathogenesis of both conditions. Treatment and prevention protocols rest on this fact. Public health policy endorses the strategies that have been repeatedly shown to be effective in managing and reducing the risks and suffering related to HIV syndemic conditions. These strategies include public health education, housing programs, family reunification, harm reduction, addiction counselling, ART, and methadone replacement therapy (Conway et al. 2005; Ehrmann 2002; Hilton et al. 2001; Riley et al. 1999; Wilson et al. 2007).

In contrast, juridical models of HIV/AIDS and addiction rest on assumptions of individual irresponsibility and criminality. These models are based on expectations of sustainable and rapid recovery that is often clinically impossible. In fact, juridical responses to HIV and addiction tend to impair rather than enable healing and health (Acker

2002; Ingram 2008; Jürgens et al. 2009). Each relapse is labelled a failure. Failure signals deficiency. Deficiency demands discipline. Discipline requires surveillance and sanction. Surveillance and sanction inculcate fear and anger. Fear and anger depress immune systems and trigger addiction relapse. And so it goes, with ever higher levels of fear and anger drawing proportionately greater degrees of surveillance and sanction.

Public health policies do not hold the same political sway that criminal justice policies do. At the time of this research, political priority was given to what Sherry Ortner (2016, 56) identifies as "punitive governance," meaning social control through fear and punishment. In 2007, Canada's National Drug Policy, which positioned addiction and HIV as health issues, was replaced with the Conservative Party's National Anti-Drug Strategy. This strategy was heralded in the 2008 federal election as proof that then Prime Minister Stephen Harper was "cleaning up drug crime." The policy diverted significant federal funds away from HIV and addiction treatment and into law enforcement (Herie and Skinner 2010, 206). An editorial in the *National Review of Medicine* condemned the strategy as anti-health and anti-science: "The new Anti-Drug Strategy is a dangerous step backwards in the fight against HIV/AIDS. Its focus on law enforcement has potential to further increase HIV and other blood-borne infections.... The focus on law enforcement will also likely prompt a rise in the incarceration rates of IDUs [injection drug users], with marginalized populations, particularly Aboriginal peoples, being hardest hit" (DeBeck et al. 2007).

Despite sharp critique, the strategy helped to secure the Harper government's re-election by tapping into a popularly held view that addiction is synonymous with moral deficiency. This was not good news for the AIDS Saskatoon PWAS, who faced increased criminalization as a result. The pernicious cycle of relapse and punishment was reinforced. Eileen described this cycle as an inescapable steel trap. "It's like on the trap lines, the animals don't get out of those traps alive," she explained. "You got to drug yourself up so that you don't feel the trap. Whenever I feel caught, I start using again so that I don't feel nothing." Rachel similarly noted that she did not necessarily use drugs to achieve a high but to experience a respite from the sense of failing and deficiency: "I need to feel nothing. But after feeling nothing comes the storm. And I feel even worse than before. So I go back to the drugs to make it stop. I can't stop going in this sad circle."

As the research participants discussed their sense of deficiency, they referenced feelings of sadness and shame. Janice noted, for example, that "it's like sadness is choking me whenever I think that [the social worker] doesn't think I'm good enough for my girls." Research participants believe that these experiences of sadness and shame are largely unintelligible to those living in different contexts. "It's real hard for [non-users] to believe," Isabel claimed, "but using [drugs] and drinking is the only thing that stopped the pain and worrying. Other people don't get that I had no other way to get by, especially when I got scared that I'd lose my daughter ... and then Mark.... Then I'd get sober and I'd feel worthless and shameful."

Shame and sadness are isolating emotions. Those who experience them often withdraw from social situations, reduce their levels of self-care (including health-related care), and increase their use of avoidant coping strategies (such as alcohol and drug use). Isolation begets more isolation, which in turn exacerbates feelings of shame and sadness. This cycle takes a painful toll on AIDS Saskatoon mothers. It not only puts their individual health at risk but limits their already restricted sources of social and material support. They turn to each other as often as they can. "Us 601 moms, we're family," Rachel said simply when I asked her whom she relies on most to help her through the difficult times. But as shame and sadness intensify, some women lose touch even with each other.

Indigeneity is seen by the PWAS at AIDS Saskatoon to be particularly significant in experiences and perceptions of deficiency. As a Euro-Canadian and HIV-positive mother, Michaela recognizes that the sadness and shame she experiences is both similar to and different from that felt by the Indigenous mothers in The 601. "It hurts so bad to feel like you're not good enough for your kid," she explained. "I try to stay healthy, but it's not always possible. And I feel so embarrassed that I'm sick. I know that Fran knows what I'm talking about. But it's worse for her because it comes with more baggage, you know? I mean, the racist stuff that's been dogging her for her whole life. It goes way back." Francine prided herself on her ability to understand the emotional experiences of other mothers while simultaneously acknowledging the differences that she felt matter most: "I feel it here [in my heart] whenever I see my friends feeling so sad because they're sick and scared they're gonna lose their kids. But us Aboriginal moms, the sadness is on our skin and it burns real bad. Our scars might not hurt any worse but they're different."

The potential loss of a child figures prominently in the women's descriptions of the relapse and convalescence associated with addiction and HIV. The loss of parental rights is an ever-present threat and a key feature of the punitive governance that structures the research participants' lives. It fuels a debilitating sense of deprivation and deficiency. In several cases, the debilitation grew to be too much to endure. Twenty-five years ago, Isabel temporarily lost custody of her daughter: "I was driving to my sister's place and I was too high and drunk. [My daughter] could have died. It was right that they took her so she could be safe. But I wish they could have placed her with my sister instead of so far away. The days away from her were so bad.... It was like I was dead, but was still in pain. I ended up in the psych ward but I don't hardly remember nothing about it there. I was just gone."

Isabel participated in the photovoice component of the research that involved taking pictures of the people, places, and things that best represent what it means to be a mother or father amidst the HIV/AIDS syndemic in Saskatchewan. When we met to discuss her pictures, Isabel began with the photograph of a dead black bear. The bear had been killed, its paws cut off, and its carcass thrown on the side of the road. Isabel stared at the photograph for a long time: "This is the first thing I've ever seen that is like how I felt when I lost my daughter. It was like I had no hands to hold her with. Like I was cut up, dead and rotting on the road, and everybody could see but nobody did nothing." She has carried this despair for over twenty-five years.

Nine of the thirty mothers who participated in this research experienced the kind of privation and despair that Isabel described. Six were hospitalized. Two women died. Derived from the Latin word *prīvātiō*, "privation" refers to the absence of that which is normally seen to be part of a person, animal, or object. A bear without its paws and a mother without hands or feet represent the loss of that which is seen as necessary to function, to fulfill vital social roles, and even to live. It is, as the root of the word implies, a private loss. It defies description. "I don't know what else to say," Isabel whispered as she continued to stare at the photograph. "I remember in counselling, they wanted me to say how I felt. I couldn't find no words. I wish I had this picture to show them."

This dimension of loss is a form of abject motherhood, a concept influenced strongly by the work of philosopher and literary critic Julia Kristeva (1982). "Abjection" refers to the degradation of an individual's sense of self to the point that they come to represent that which is abhorred. The culturally abject individual stands in sharp contrast to the venerated. In her study of militarized motherhood in Turkey, Senem Kaptan (2011, 260) argues that many political institutions and social systems cast motherhood dichotomously as either exemplary or abject. The nine research participants who experienced privation have had their status as mothers degraded to the point that they are often seen by others, and come to see themselves, as abject. This may be why Isabel found the photograph of the mutilated bear so powerful. This may also be why Isabel and eight other AIDS Saskatoon mothers described their privational despair with metaphors of bodily dismemberment.

Nancy suffered unbearable despair when her niece was removed from her care. "[My niece] and me were always together," she explained. "Losing her is like getting my heart gouged out of me." As the non-biological mother to the twelve-year-old in her care, Nancy was cast as particularly abject. "I think my doctors look at me like I'm crazy," she said. "They think that because I'm not [my niece's] mother, I can't love her like she's mine or cry over losing her. It's like I don't have ... human feelings." After her brother, Johnny, took a job in the oil fields of Alberta, Nancy offered to take care of her niece so the girl could stay in Saskatoon with family. Nancy's boyfriend painted the second bedroom in their apartment a bright shade of purple. A woman from the neighbouring church gave them a frilly white quilt for the girl's bed. Theresa spent the weekend helping Nancy clean the apartment and Isabel bought all the fixings for a favourite meal (hamburger soup, bannock, and apple pie). Two days after Nancy's niece moved in, she was removed and placed in a foster home until Johnny could return. Nancy's HIV-status, former involvement in sex work, and drug use rendered her "unfit."

I did not see Nancy again after we last spoke about her niece. Several PWAS in The 601 told me that they were worried about her. She had withdrawn from her friends, turning inward in ways she had not done before. Johnny attended the public exhibit of the photovoice images and mentioned Nancy. He had never seen her like this, saying,

"She's always been the happy one of all of us kids. But losing [my daughter] after she promised she'd take care of her, well, that hurt her in a way that only other girls with HIV can know. The hate out in the world is a real thing. It's vicious.... And Nance took it bad." I will never know the extent to which this despair figured into Nancy's death five years later. Privation never fully subsides. It combines with deprivation and deficiency to intensify grief, rendering it unrelenting.

The Saskatchewan HIV/AIDS syndemic creates a hostile environment for HIV-affected mothers, one in which their maternal fitness and their right to grieve for the children removed from their care are questioned and denied. Their health conditions are increasingly criminalized while health resources are reduced. They are held individually responsible for the circumstances of their lives as the structural forces that create their environments recede from public and political view. AIDS Saskatoon mothers report being viewed by service providers and members of the broader public not as aggrieved victims of structural injustice but as wilful and contaminated criminals. In this context, the emotional responses to loss constitute a private and culturally specific suffering. AIDS Saskatoon mothers often feel that they have only each other as they grieve, and some die, for the children in their lives.

CONCLUSION

Catherine Lutz (1998, 225) argues that "rather than modeling people as either thinking *or* feeling, we might view people as almost always emotional." Nearly everyone is passionately involved in the world, even when those passions simmer beneath what appear to be external and seemingly cool decisions. The challenge for anthropologists is to tap into, systematically record, and fairly represent those passions. It allows for an intimate, person-centred, and culturally grounded understanding of emotion. However, as much as we learn about emotions in an abstract and vicarious sense, no one can ever actually experience another person's emotion. We cannot fully access the sensory response that someone else is having to a painful, stressful, or joyful situation. We can, however, pay attention to the pauses, tears, interruptions, repetitions, and metaphors that fill our conversations. We can situate experiences in relation to the general human capacity for emotion as well as the particular cultural and political terrains that shape emotional expression.

Anthropologists counterbalance the psychometric research on emotion and HIV with detailed and locally grounded case studies and stories. "The experience of suffering," physician and anthropologist Paul Farmer (2004, 31) explains, "is not effectively conveyed by statistics or graphs.... The 'texture' of dire affliction is better felt in the gritty details of biography." His telling of Acéphie Joseph's life in Haiti is unforgettable. Acéphie was a "water refugee." She was born in a desperately poor settlement that was established after the construction of Haiti's largest dam flooded out farming communities. Acéphie grew up with little schooling, no health care, and a bleak future. She hoped that marriage would provide some economic security, but her two relationships did not last. Her first romance with an already married soldier was brief, and he died shortly after their relationship ended. Her second boyfriend left her after learning she was pregnant. Acéphie's baby stretched her family's ability to provide food and shelter to the breaking point. Things only grew worse:

> Within months of her daughter's birth, Acéphie's life was consumed with managing her own drenching night sweats and debilitating diarrhea while attempting to care for her child. "We both need diapers now," she remarked bitterly towards the end of her life.... As she became more and more gaunt, some villagers suggested that Acéphie was the victim of sorcery.... Acéphie herself knew that she had AIDS although she was more apt to refer to herself as suffering from a disorder brought on by work as a servant. "All that ironing, and then opening a refrigerator." She died far from refrigerators or other amenities as her family stood by helplessly. (35)

This is not only Acéphie's story. It is also a story of emotion and family. "The pain of Acéphie's mother and twin brother was manifestly intense," Farmer points out. "But few understood her father's anguish. Shortly after Acéphie's death, he hanged himself with a length of rope" (35).

Farmer asserts that this story is not anecdotal. "In the eyes of the epidemiologist," he writes, "[Acéphie] suffered and died in exemplary fashion. Millions of people living in similar circumstances can expect to meet similar fates. What these victims share are not personal or psychological attributes.... What they share, rather, is the experience of occupying the bottom rung of the social ladder in inegalitarian societies" (31). The stories that the research participants shared with me and each other are similarly illustrative. Their emotional responses to illness, punitive governance, and structural inequity are often shared by Indigenous Peoples across the world. Simultaneously, though, their emotional experiences of loss are specific to the local realities of the Saskatchewan HIV syndemic. It is significant that research participants did not discuss grief and mourning in relation to culturally venerated traditions. They did not mention the ceremonies, Spirit visions, dancing, or dreams that have long been included in the mourning rituals of many First Nations Peoples (LivingMyCulture 2016; Spiwak et al. 2012). They did not situate their losses in relation to hunting cycles or rhythms of the land as was traditionally done in Cree and Ojibway nations (Hackett 2005). Instead, AIDS Saskatoon mothers situate and experience the anger and fear of deprivation, the shame and sadness of deficiency, and the despair of privation within a more recent and localized history of child apprehension and HIV-related stigma. They reach to their parents' generation and their youth in addition to the here-and-now to make sense of the seemingly unrelenting threat of child apprehension.

In my last interview with Rachel, she connected her own struggle with that of her mother: "My mom ... she drank herself to death 'cause residential school broke her, 'cause us kids got taken away from her. She used to talk about the sadness. [She] said it was like falling through the ice and freezing up and drowning.... Turns out she drowned herself with booze.... But she had to find warmth some place, you know? The bottle did it for her. And God knows enough [people] pushed her to the place where that was all she had."

Rachel's mother died of alcohol-related illnesses. In Rachel's remembrances, her mother could well have died of grief for a Cree mother's life that she could not live. "What do you see in your own future as a mother?" I asked. "I don't know," she replied. "I don't want to go the way my mom did. I don't want *mescinewin* to win." After a long silence, she added, "I guess us AIDS moms got to find a way to make our love count for something."

6 Love

> Places, like voices, are local and multiple. For each inhabitant, a place has a unique reality, one in which meaning is shared with other people and places. The links in these chains of experienced places are forged of culture and history.
>
> – *Margaret Rodman (1992, 643)*

I received an especially warm greeting in The 601 when I arrived for my meeting with Susan. "I'm so happy to see you!" Isabel said with a smile. "I hope your interview with Sue takes a *long* time so I don't got to listen to her sing anymore." Susan was helping the volunteers clean the coffee area. As she worked, she was loudly singing the theme song to the 1970s hit television show *Happy Days*: "Thursday, Friday, happy daaaays, groovin' all week with yooou." The new Classic TV cable channel in The 601 had quickly become a favourite. A young man called out, "Sorry to tell you this, Ma, but you ain't no Beyoncé!" We all laughed when he then started to sing along. Many of the younger PWAS in The 601 see Susan as a mother. "Eileen and me ooze mama love," Susan cheerily explained. "The kids come running and it's win-win. Good for them 'cause they know we look out for them. And good for us 'cause it keeps us going. Gives us something to stay healthy for."

Susan is originally from a northern Dene community. She left home when she was sixteen and has been living in Saskatoon for the past

Photo 2. Susan's neighbourhood cat

twenty-seven years. She has a presence that fills a room. Her laugh is loud. Her stories are animated. Her memory for personal detail is unparalleled. She makes a special effort to remember the favourite foods, music, and television shows of everyone in The 601: "I know what it's like to feel like human garbage and I don't want nobody feeling like that." Susan proudly claims a "block mother" role for herself in the neighbourhood, reaching out to everyone in need.

All but one of the photographs that Susan took for the photovoice component of this research focused on neighbourhood features that represent home. She particularly liked the photograph of a little white cat in the alley beside her house (Photo 2). "I have to really watch this cat," she explained. "He'll take off and run away so I have to watch him all the time. I don't mind, though. I love animals and kids."

When I asked about the debris pictured in the photograph, Susan said, "Yeah, condoms, garbage, [cigarette] butts, they're all over this place. But what can you do? It's still home." Susan does her best to take care of the neighbourhood. She clears the litter from the front of the church where those without secure housing take shelter. She brings food to the young women who work in the local sex trades, as Susan herself once did. She knows the police officers and drug dealers by name, and she is respected by both groups. The neighbourhood is, as Susan stated once more, "still home."

This chapter explores how the connection between love and home is forged by those living with and affected by HIV/AIDS. This connection is sustained against great odds. Almost 60 per cent of research participants have never lived anywhere for longer than five years. Rental property in Saskatoon is expensive and housing programs are often short lived. Landlords and property managers tend to reject potential renters and evict current tenants who are known to be HIV-positive and have addiction issues. Racism makes it particularly difficult for the Indigenous research participants to find safe and secure housing. A 2015 advertisement for an available rental property, for example, ran with the heading "No Natives, Please." The text of the ad indicated that newcomers to Canada were welcome "but aboriginals will not be considered" (CBC News 2015). The ad drew public outcry and was removed. However, many Indigenous people in Saskatchewan report facing similar and ongoing (if less public) discrimination from property owners and managers.

Despite the difficulties with securing adequate housing, 85 per cent of research participants describe feeling "at home" in the neighbourhood around AIDS Saskatoon. "If I got to stay here in Saskatoon," Isabel said, "I want to stay right where I live now. We have family all around. The 601 is here ... and Mark knows he's safe." Sally also wants to stay in her current home because "it's a real safe street. Me and the neighbours want it to stay that way. This is where we're a family. It's where we take care of each other." Almost all of the mothers who participated in this research shared lively and detailed stories about the homes that hold memories of their children, family, and daily life. Susan spoke most frequently about it, saying, "You can't just stay inside. You got to get out and make a home all around.... Home is where the kids are loved and where you can sing as loud as you want." With that, she burst into song again. Isabel called to us from the AIDS Saskatoon kitchen, "I can still hear you!"

Many residents and business owners who share the neighbourhood with AIDS Saskatoon tell a different story. In June 2012, a public meeting was called at a local library to address concerns about the needle exchange program that runs out of The 601. The then executive director of AIDS Saskatoon explained to the press that the program had been running for three and a half years. It is one of the quietest in the city, operating only three afternoons per week and exchanging an average of two needles per day (Warren 2012b, B7). I attended the neighbourhood meeting with several members of AIDS Saskatoon's Board and the CAC for this research. A panel of speakers – including the Saskatoon Health Region's deputy medical officer (also an HIV specialist), two police officers, two local business owners, and the executive director of AIDS Saskatoon – made presentations and answered questions from the crowd. The police officers explained that although property crime in the area had increased, it was associated more with the local bars than with The 601. Violent crime had decreased. AIDS Saskatoon's executive director presented evidence showing that the number of discarded needles found during clean-up campaigns had decreased since the needle exchange opened. The medical officer concurred, adding that the risk of contracting HIV from a discarded needle is extremely low.

The crowd was not convinced. One woman interrupted the speakers to declare, "I'm a loving grandmother and I have to wade through knee-high needles to pick my grandson up from school. Every day I think I'm going to get AIDS and die." A local business owner said that the PWAS have "dirty clothes and spread disease." Another woman stood up and asked, "Who has more rights, the residents or the drug users?" Thinking of the women who participated in this research, I tried to point out that, like other concerned residents, the mothers who access the services at AIDS Saskatoon love their children and want to contribute to their community. The loving grandmother shouted me down: "I don't want those animals destroying our homes. They're incapable of loving anyone." The man sitting beside her agreed, claiming that "they got no right to be here." This drew sharp rebuke from members of the AIDS Saskatoon Board. The hostility in the room grew. When the city councillor who represented the neighbourhood spoke in support of AIDS Saskatoon's programs and PWAS, she was loudly jeered.

HIV-related stigma, like all stigmas, not only marks those who are deemed to be undesirable. It also separates social realms of safety from sites of perceived danger. Nancy Scheper-Hughes (1993, 374) explains that the expression of stigma "involves all those exclusionary, dichotomous contradictions that allow us to draw safe boundaries around the acceptable, the permissible, the desirable, so as to contain our own fears and phobias about sickness, death and decay." When those who are stigmatized come too close to the designated realms of safety, those fears and phobias can cause considerable conflict. Erving Goffman (1963, 13), arguably the most influential theorist of stigma, refers to this kind of conflict encounter as a sociological primal scene. Uncertainties and anger loom large. Accounts of dangers are exaggerated. Incidental improprieties among the stigmatized (such as clothes that appear dirty) are interpreted as signs of irredeemable deficiency.

A sociological primal scene unfolded to script at the neighbourhood meeting on that June evening. PWAS were cast as dangerous harbingers of disease. The few syringes found on the streets became knee-deep piles. AIDS and death were deemed imminent. "Drug users" had no "rightful" place in the community. Granted, there were some residents who did not share these views. One woman who had lived in the area for many years enjoyed meeting AIDS Saskatoon PWAS and staff. "It seems like all of this [concern] has come about because people just found out that the needle exchange exists," she told a local reporter (Warren 2012a, A3). The majority of meeting-goers, however, expressed their opposition to AIDS Saskatoon's programs and PWAS through a singular and stigmatizing narrative of "us" and "other": resident and drug user, healthy and diseased, acceptable and unacceptable, safe and dangerous, loving and heartless.

Sociologist Howard Becker (1963), a contemporary of Erving Goffman, would likely describe these meeting-goers as "moral entrepreneurs." They identify what they see as sources of danger, and they express dissatisfaction with existing rules to contain and quell all associated risk. According to Becker (147–8), moral entrepreneurs act publicly to make and enforce a different set of rules. They embrace an "absolute ethic" that discounts information and excludes experiences that are inconsistent with their own views and aims. Despite the information presented by police and medical officers, many meeting-goers clung tightly to their view that HIV and drug use are a menacing and imminent threat to their safety and community. Their stories did not acknowledge or accommodate the presence or contributions of AIDS Saskatoon mothers, like Susan, who have a genuine investment in the community.

For over half a century since Goffman's and Becker's work first appeared, sociologists have explored how absolute ethics define social issues and inform the institutional responses to them. During this period, anthropologists have made it a priority to attend to the stories that are silenced by stigma. We argue that no story or experience is ever truly singular. We therefore focus on what Margaret Rodman (1992) calls the multivocality of experience and the multilocality of place. I join this discussion through the AIDS Saskatoon research by exploring the stories of maternal love and home that unfold alongside those of the moral entrepreneurs. "I know that a lot of people don't want us here," Susan explained in a rare moment of frustration. "But I raised my son here. I love him so much, and I don't ever want to lose him. So, my heart lives here."

"IT'S LIKE I WAS SPEAKING A DIFFERENT LANGUAGE": LOVE AND RISK

Social media become abuzz every Mother's Day with celebrations of motherly love. One of the most popular memes, credited to author Marion Garrety, reads "Mother love is the fuel that enables a normal human being to do the impossible." Stories of mothers doing the impossible and displaying superhuman strength have indeed become legendary. In 2006, Lydia Angiyou of Ivujivuk, Quebec, tackled and successfully fought off a polar bear in order to save her son and two other children (George 2006). Angela Cavallo of Lawrenceville, Georgia, single-handedly lifted a Chevy Impala off her teenaged son when the jacks supporting the car buckled. Cavallo's story continues to be featured in popular magazines decades after the 1982 incident (Beck 2011). As Shari Thurer (1994, xvi) states, "Mother love is powerful stuff."

As discussed, AIDS Saskatoon mothers are often accused of not loving their children. The accusation goes so far as to assert that HIV-affected mothers are not capable of love. In order to assess the effects of this insidious accusation, it is important to turn to the century-long investigation into what motherly love actually is. The focus of this investigation has largely been on the biological and hormonal basis of mother-infant bonding. We now know that the neuropeptide oxytocin is released with intimate physical contact and close emotional connection, earning it the moniker "the love hormone." It fosters social bonding and psychological stability. It can increase empathy and decrease anxiety (Neumann 2007). Oxytocin plays a significant role in mother-child bonding. It not only helps to regulate childbirth and lactation, it also enhances the pleasure sensation of mother-infant contact (Galbally et al. 2011). This leads to better maternal and child health, not only during the peri- and post-partum periods but, in some cases, for as long as a close mother-child relationship is maintained.

Oxytocin, however, does not *cause* social bonding. It creates a biological propensity for it. Animal studies indicate that social environments must simultaneously foster and sustain conditions that allow bonding to take place. A team of neurobiologists at New York University's School of Medicine, for example, has found that higher levels of oxytocin in female mice increase their ability to recognize and then respond to the cries of distressed pups (Martin et al. 2015). Mice do not instinctively know when or how to retrieve their crying infants; other mice must teach them. The researchers show that increasing levels of oxytocin affects behaviour because it heightens the awareness of females to relevant social cues, allowing them to learn and adopt response behaviours more quickly. The social environment of mice, therefore, is as important to the bonding between mothers and pups as individual neurobiology.

The advanced cultural systems of humans make the social environments that enable or constrain mother-child bonding even more influential. There must be cultural, institutional, and interpersonal support for the loving behaviours that are key to mother-child bonding. Despite the sentimental Mother's Day memes and legendary stories of maternal strength, however, public support has been in short supply since the mid-twentieth century. Molly Ladd-Taylor (2007, 663) explains that World War II was a turning point when mothering and maternal love went from being viewed as virtuous to being condemned as treacherous: "The positive image of the virtuous mother who made the supreme sacrifice by sending her sons off to war was displaced by the domineering 'Mom' who kept them tied to her apron strings and – according to the U.S. psychiatrist Edward Strecker – caused an alarming instance of psychoneuroses in servicemen.... Cold War anxieties accelerated the mother-bashing frenzy. Smothering stay-at-home moms were accused of turning their sons into homosexuals or communists, working mothers of producing juvenile delinquents, and Black 'matriarchs' of causing Black men's unemployment and poverty."

Medical historian Anne Harrington (2016) points out that the social "problems" of the day, such as civil unrest in the 1970s and urban crime in the 1990s, are not usually seen as issues of social inequity or institutional failure. They are more frequently and publicly portrayed as products of individual dysfunction borne of inadequate mothering. Over fifty years ago, psychologist John Watson claimed that society suffers because of powerful and pathological maternal love: "Mother love is a dangerous instrument.... Mothers today are incompetent. Most should be indicted for psychological murder" (cited in Hymowitz 2003, 52). This is not a bygone sentiment. The politically conservative news coverage of the 2011 riots in Britain included plenty of conjecture about the deficient motherly care and love the rioters received as children (Bristow 2013). On the other end of the political spectrum, many of the liberal-leaning critiques of the 2017 alt-right, white supremacist protests in Charlottesville, Virginia, dubbed the mothers of racist protestors as "ultimately accountable" for the "monsters" they created through a lack of emotion or concern (Chainey 2017).

The preoccupation with the dangers of maternal love intensifies the rhetoric of mother blame as well as the professionalization of motherhood. Psychologist Paula Caplan recalls that she became interested in mother blame through her work in a hospital clinic. "No matter what was wrong, no matter what the reason for the family's coming to the clinic," Caplan (2007, 592) claims, "it turned out the mother was always assumed to be responsible for the problem." As one of the leading theorists in the field, she argues that the standards of motherhood are so onerous and the judgment of mothers so severe that women are frightened, devalued, and exhausted. Studies across the social sciences demonstrate that mothers tend to be "rendered invisible when they are succeeding but are berated for any work they fail to do – or cannot do – in a perfect manner" (Reimer and Sahagian 2015, 4).

The more mothers are blamed for causing harm to their children and to society, the more they are deemed to need expert guidance. Maternal love is a favourite target for all kinds of experts who hope to profit from the parenting advice industry by transforming love from an emotion to a trainable skill. Expert advice on how to express maternal love, however, has rarely endured the test of time. Psychiatrists were once absolutely certain of the dangers associated with kissing a baby. Mothers were advised to limit themselves to one kiss on the child's forehead per day. They should otherwise shake hands with their children to show affection (Watson and Watson 1928). In the 1930s, pregnant women were told that in order to have a loveable baby, they should "avoid thinking of ugly people, or those marked by deformity or disease" (O'Neil 2013). Doctors in the 1950s and 1960s occasionally recommended giving "sleepy babies" (as young as six months old) coffee or cola. After all, a loving mother would want to stimulate curiosity (Sacket 1962). In the same period, mothers were advised to use tranquilizers to calm active or anxious children. There would be no adverse side effects, mothers were assured, as long as the medication was given with love (Hardyment 1995). It is easy to view this advice as nonsensical and outdated but, as historian Rima Apple (2006) argues, it was leading-edge knowledge at the time. Mothers were encouraged and, in some cases, required to heed it.

An expert-driven environment continues to set standards for maternal love. Unlike in the past, though, many women today can be more discerning. Mothers have unprecedented agency in selecting the advice that fits best with their life. However, according to Ellie Lee and colleagues (2014), mothers are apt to seek and accept advice more quickly and less judiciously when it concerns the identification and reduction of risk. Like maternal love, risk has consequently become a lucrative sector within the parenting advice industry. Children are now "defined as *de facto* 'at risk,' but what exactly the 'risk' *is* is often uncertain or unknown. It is a 'worst case scenario,' a possibility rather than a probability" (Lee et al. 2014, 11). With danger supposedly lurking around every corner, mothers must be more vigilant in protecting their children than ever before. Joan Wolf (2011, xv) explains that mothers are now held "responsible for matters well outside their control, and they are told in various ways that they must eliminate even minute, ultimately ineradicable, potential threats to their children's well-being."

This supposedly ever-present risk creates a difficult environment for all mothers. It is particularly difficult for mothers who are poor, ill, addicted, and culturally marginalized. These women often find themselves cast as agents of danger rather than maternal love. They are the "others" against whom the moral entrepreneurs crusade. The risks that these mothers face are rendered invisible, while the risks that they supposedly pose draw critical attention. "Those animals are *not* like me and they *do not* care for their children," the loving grandmother asserted as she loudly left the June neighbourhood meeting.

AIDS Saskatoon mothers navigate fear and risk every day. The risks that they face are not vague possibilities. Addiction relapse, poverty, housing insecurity, child apprehension, racism, and treatment side effects (such as liver damage, heart disease, bone loss, and internal bleeding) pose very real threats to their well-being. Even the common cold can be a serious danger to those with HIV-compromised immune systems. Working to reduce the probability of harm takes substantial effort. "But there's no other option," Janice explained after listing a litany of risks that she routinely confronts. "My kids need me. And I love them so much.... I got no other choice but to do what needs to get done." Rachel explained that dealing with the daily risks associated with the HIV syndemic in Saskatchewan is both necessary and exhausting, saying, "It's like a gamble every day. You gotta figure out the odds that you'll get sick or somebody will hate on you 'cause you got tracks on your arm, 'cause you're Native, 'cause you got HIV or hep C.... But every day you got to work to beat them odds. That's what you got to do when you love your kids. I don't know nobody who doesn't know that. And I don't know nobody who's not dead tired from it."

AIDS Saskatoon mothers associate risk management with maternal love just as other mothers do. However, they rarely indulge general "what if" scenarios. The women who participated in this research referenced specific dangers when asked about the safety of their children. Susan is among the majority of participants who define HIV-related stigma, child apprehension, and illness as the three most pressing risks for mothers and their children, saying, "I'm most scared of how people treat our kids.... The haters come out, yelling at the kids, treating them real bad. I'm scared of the kid-snatching [social service] people. You saw what they did to Isabel. They just took Mark away and nobody could love that kid more than her. I'm scared that I'll get too sick to take care of things around here. The kids here need me. If I'm not around, if I get too sick ... they don't do so good. They need love."

Over 90 per cent of the research participants responded with frustration and confusion when asked to address the vaguely defined risks that concern service providers and neighbours. Rachel recalled the conversation that she had with the caseworker who was conducting her parental assessment, "She goes, 'what are you doing to keep [the boys] safe? I say, 'safe from what?' She goes, 'from everything.' I go, 'I don't let nobody hurt them.' She goes, 'yeah, but how do you keep them *generally* safe?' And I go, 'safe from what?'" This exchange apparently went on for a while. Rachel continued, "I told her that I feed them good. I take them to school every morning and their uncle picks them up every afternoon when I'm at work. She kept saying, 'That's not what I mean.' Well, *shiiiit*, lady, what *do* you mean then?"

Michaela responded with similar frustration when she was suspected of neglecting her daughter. Michaela had mistakenly left her television on while she was out at her friend's party, "I guess my neighbour heard the TV and thought I'd just left [my daughter] there alone, which I never do. [My daughter] was with her dad and his mom. She was perfectly safe." Fearing that the child was unattended, Michaela's neighbour called the police. "When I got home, and yeah, I was high, the cops were waiting," Michaela recalled. She continued, "Then the nightmare started.... The social workers got involved. [My daughter] had to stay with my ex's mom while they 'assess the situation.' I got right in my neighbour's face about it, you know? '[My daughter] was totally safe so there was no reason to call the cops. *No reason*.' She says, 'If you loved your kid, you'd keep her safe. You wouldn't put her in danger.' I yelled, 'What danger?' And she says, '*Everything* is dangerous.' What the hell does that even mean?"

As discussed in Chapter 4, a miscommunication often occurs when health care providers are seeking specific medical information and research participants respond with broad discussions about social context and historical realities. The miscommunication around safety involves a comparable conflict between the specific and the general. In this case, though, it is the research participants who focus on specificities and are at a loss as to how to address the vague dangers that moral entrepreneurs associate with the HIV syndemic. "I love [my daughter] so much and I know how to keep her safe," Michaela exclaimed. "But when I tried to explain to [my neighbour], the police, and the social workers, they didn't want to hear about all the things I do. It's like they couldn't hear me. It's like I was speaking a different language." Francine agreed emphatically: "It's like the people who don't know anything about us hate us because we aren't just like them. It's like they want our stories to be the same as theirs. But our stories are different and they'd know that if they listened."

Michaela and Francine are among the twenty-four women who, through the course of the research, expressed concern that they are not given the narrative freedom to describe how maternal love figures in their lives and informs the care they provide to their children. "When [my neighbour] said, 'If you really loved your kid, you'd keep her safe,' it was like she had already decided that I didn't love [my daughter]," Michaela said, choking back tears. "It was like she put her hands over her ears and wouldn't listen to anything I had to say."

If the research participants could tell their maternal love story as they wanted, unencumbered by the absolute ethics of moral entrepreneurs, how would it begin and unfold? Research participants unanimously agreed that their story should begin "at home."

"A GOOD PLACE TO PUT THE LOVE": HOME

"Here's the first house I ever lived in here in Saskatoon," Susan said proudly as she looked at the photo (Photo 3). "I lived in three apartments and one boarding house before that. But this is the first house. [My son's] dad put a swing on the tree in the back yard. I used to sit out there and watch [my son] swing back and forth." After singing two choruses of "All You Need Is Love," she turned her attention back to the photo:

> We lived in this house when I got told that I got HIV. I had been [using drugs] on and off for a couple of years, eh? I never let [my son] see me or nothing like that.... But there was some real dark times. The doctor at the hospital told me I got HIV, and I got so scared. I came home to this house and I crawled into bed. I felt real safe, tucked in with the people I love coming and going. After my son's dad and me split ... we moved. But I sure loved that house.

As discussed in the introductory chapter, photovoice is a methodology that privileges the image-based dimension of narrative, letting participants visually represent aspects of their lives through photography. This has transformative potential. African American studies scholar Leigh Raiford (2011, 15) argues that photography has been central to civil rights struggles because it provides a way "to define and represent oneself as one chooses and a freedom from the ideological and material consequences of dehumanizing depictions." Photographers can challenge the stigmatizing and distorting images others have created of them. Raiford (2011, 3) also points out, however, that photographs can imprison those they represent by creating fixed images that foreclose on social change. Although anthropologists address both the empowering and limiting dimensions of any image, Susan Levine (2003) argues that we can best serve our community partners by prioritizing the empowering potential of visual imagery.

The six women and seven men who participated in the photovoice component of this research took a total of 234 photographs. They described all but five of the photographs in positive terms, referring to the sense of engagement, well-being, and safety that the images represent. The photographs were analyzed in two stages. First, participants assigned each photograph to one of three main categories: 107 photographs of people; 81 photographs of place; and 46 photographs of human-made things. In the second stage of analysis, photographs were assigned to as many categories as the participants deemed relevant. Almost half of the photographs ended up in more than one category and the total counts increased: 122 photographs include people, 121 depict place, and 96 include things.

Photo 3. Susan's first house

Although the research participants took more photographs of people, they were more likely to discuss parental love in their responses to images of place. This was particularly the case in the interviews with mothers. Pictures of houses, parks, buildings, and streets prompted twice as many descriptions of maternal love than photographs of people did. This may be because place often encompasses kin networks and community belonging. Everyday life does not unfold in a neutral location. Our environments influence, and are influenced by, our aesthetics, emotions, experiences, health, and politics. Whereas the term *space* refers to abstract locations that have no socially shared significance, *place* is rich with cultural meaning and emotional connections. Place, Sarah Pink (2012, 5) states, is "where we make our worlds and our worlds make us."

Home is a place that carries particular significance. Neuroanthropologist John Allen begins his book on human habitats by arguing that as a species we are not so much home*bodies* as we are home*minded*. "Home is not simply a location on the landscape where a person lives; it has a privileged place in our cognition," Allen (2015, 1–2) asserts. "Home brings on feelings of comfort, security, and control.... When we say we 'feel at home,' it means something important." It is possible, therefore, to feel at home in various places and differing ways. Isabel's reaction to the photograph she took of the horses on her home reserve (Photo 4) illustrates this well. "Look at them beautiful horses," she exclaimed. "That makes my heart feel at peace. My roots are there. Always will be. Home here [in Saskatoon] is good but it's different. It's just real special out there."

Photo 4. Horses on Isabel's home reserve

Isabel plans to stay in Saskatoon because she can access HIV care and addictions counselling. She can take care of her daughter and remain the primary caregiver to Mark. She can continue working. But as much as her Saskatoon home offers, her home reserve holds a special sense of peace.

Ten of the thirteen photovoice participants and thirty-five of the participants across all components of this research made repeated references to a home reserve that was a site of comfort and well-being. Descriptions of "having roots," a sense of historical groundedness and cultural belonging, arose most frequently. "I got lots of rez family," Rachel explained. "It's real easy to feel the love there [and] to feel like you got a history." Although Charlotte can rarely afford to return to her home reserve in Manitoba, she also recalled the comfort and love: "Saskatoon is home for me now, for sure. But on the reserve, I just feel more settled. I feel like I can breathe easier, like I'm part of something." After her miscarriage, Lisa longed to be at home on the reserve, saying "I just wanted to be there. I always feel better and get healthy there."

Homes on the reserves are consistently described as being centred on kin and community. "Family comes first and everybody's like family," Isabel explained. "Everybody knows everybody out there and when we need something, like a new roof or something, everybody chips in to help." The experts to whom residents most commonly turn for guidance are well-known and respected members of the community. "The people here on the rez, I trust them," Isabel continued. "You don't need nobody from off rez if you're looking for help with your kids, or your farm, or whatever. The Elders and the older people here, they know what they're doing." It is interesting that as we sat together in the research office at AIDS Saskatoon, Isabel shifted from referring to the reserve as "there" and referred to it as "here." The more Isabel looked at and talked about the photo of the horse pasture outside her home on the reserve, the closer it became.

Reserve life is not painted as completely idyllic, however. Twenty of the research participants discussed encountering HIV-related stigma on their home reserves. "I got to keep my guard up around the HIV stuff," Rachel said. "It's not as bad as here in the city, but there's HIV hate there, too." Charlotte noted that "I can't say nothing about using [drugs], or having hep C or HIV, or nothing like that. I'd be real ashamed if I talked about it in Indian country." Although Isabel spoke very affectionately about her home reserve, she too had concerns. "Our chiefs talk lots about cultural revitalization in Indian country," she said. "But if you're doing things that they don't like, things that aren't part of that cultural revitalization, then there's shame there. And it's not just the drugs and HIV neither. It's the fighting and the drinking. And everything feels like it's out in the open so you can't get away with nothing.... Your family is public business on the rez. That's what makes it so good for the kids but real hard on the moms and *kohkums* who don't feel part of the cultural revitalization."

The interconnection of family and political life is common to the governance of many First Nations. The separation of public and private social realms that has permeated European societies since the Industrial Revolution has no direct corollary in most Indigenous societies. Wayne Warry (1998, 235) points out that "for Aboriginal people, removing kinship from professional affairs – indeed from 'affairs of the state' – is impossible." Indigenous public cultures entail notions of a common good and a shared kin-based heritage. Many of the mothers and fathers who participated in this research therefore feel that their HIV status and drug use detract from the collective vibrancy of reserve life. Isabel's brother, Martin, shares her love of their family's home but he too identified moments of discomfort, saying, "I love it there. The sweat lodges have helped me a lot. But when the Elders talk about traditional ways as a way to help our people on the reserve, I feel real bad. I can't break the [addiction] cycle and that's not the traditional way."

The list of ongoing problems that the colonial and state-imposed reserve system created for Indigenous Peoples in Canada is long. Substandard housing, contaminated water, insufficient land resources, inaccessible and unsafe schools, inadequate health care facilities, and youth suicide are among the most pernicious problems that reserve communities face today. The reserve system was established in western Canada shortly after the country's formation in 1867. Indigenous peoples were relocated from their traditional territories onto smaller

Photo 5. Neighbourhood library

parcels of land with more limited resources (Lux 2001). Colonial powers believed that creating a system of Indigenous dependency on the state was a necessary step in the government's assimilationist agenda. The goal, after all, was to eliminate First Nations cultural traditions and replace them with European lifeways. Reserve communities were consequently under-resourced and vulnerable to the manipulative tactics of government agents and the companies contracted to provide essential services. In his award-winning study of disease and starvation on the Canadian plains, James Daschuk (2013) documents that substandard and tainted food was provided to reserves in order to starve Indigenous populations into submission.

Despite the indelible and colonial imprint on reserve life, Indigenous Peoples across Canada are, as Isabel noted, working to decolonize their communities through cultural revitalizing efforts (among other strategies). The First Peoples' Cultural Council promotes Indigenous language revitalization as essential to these efforts (Moore and Macdonald 2013). Other aspects of culture, including traditional foods and feasts, political governance, restorative justice, residential patterns, and healing are increasingly incorporated into what Jen Bagelman and colleagues (2016, 6) refer to as "healthful revitalization." These programs offer a great deal to reserve communities. However, they rarely include HIV-related harm reduction strategies, and some actively exclude those who have enduring issues with addiction and drug use. Many of the Indigenous PWAS at AIDS Saskatoon therefore feel that there is a barrier to their full inclusion in reserve life. "I love the rez," Rachel repeated for the third time. "It's real good for the boys to get that love. But, for me, there's a push there too, pushing me away because I can't stay on the path that the community wants me to walk.... When I feel that push, I head right on back home here [in Saskatoon]."

Most research participants describe a strong connection to the Saskatoon neighbourhoods that they also consider home. George and Hayley, a couple originally from the same central Saskatchewan reserve, took a combined total of twenty-two photos of their neighbourhood. George felt that his photo of a local library (Photo 5) best reflects being a father amidst the HIV syndemic:

> This is a good place. I go there with the kids after school and before [night shift] work and we go through their homework. The librarians let us talk all we want.... It's like home.... Sometimes when we're there, I sit and look at the kids. It's like wow. My kids are *smart*. They got an old man with HIV and tracks [on his arms]. But they're smart kids. And they're good kids too.... I'm real proud of them.... I don't know if this is going to sound conceited or stupid, but I feel like I'm doing real good when I'm there with them, like I'm being the best father I can.

Hayley also took photos of the library but she chose a picture of their children's school (Photo 6) as her favourite. "My two youngest go to school here and they spend so much time there," Hayley explained. "They're away from me all day and I can't protect them. So I got to trust the teachers to do that. Trust is hard when you got hep C and HIV. It makes you an easy target. But I love my kids, so I got to trust. You got to keep a circle of trust around the kids." For most research participants, this circle of trust includes teachers, library workers, AIDS Saskatoon staff, and many PWAS.

AIDS Saskatoon mothers and fathers identify grandmothers, mothers, and children as central to their kin network. Francine explained that she took a photograph of a local street (Photo 7) because she liked the chicken restaurant. "There's always a family deal there," she noted with a smile. "If we save up and chip in, the core fourteen or fifteen of us can treat ourselves to a family night."

Francine's "core group" includes her two daughters, their four children, and her son's five children. The mothers of her son's children and one other grandmother round out the group to fifteen. Francine's son, Johnny, similarly described the photograph of his computer (Photo 8) in relation to a core group of grandmothers, mothers, and children:

> My mom doesn't know how to use [the computer].... I show her how to look at the pictures I put on there of her grandkids. She puts her hand on the screen and I see tears in her eyes. She's had such a tough life. She's been so sick for so long.... She almost died

> when she was a kid but the Creator saw a spirit in her and kept her here for us. She was on the AIDS medicines early on. Those pills were worse than the ones today and they made her real sick. But she did her best to take care of us kids, even when she was so sick.... Being a mother and *kohkum* is the centre of her whole world. The world turns around the mothers, *kohkums*, and kids.

Photo 6. Elementary school

Photo 7. Street and mall with Francine's favourite chicken restaurant

Participants across all components of this research describe their kin networks as concentric circles of care and trust. One circle is embedded in another, and a collective spirit prevails. Mothers, grandmothers, and children constitute the innermost circle. Moving outward from the matrifocal centre, the second circle includes aunts and fathers. Raylynne, a twenty-eight-year-old mother of three, explained that "the aunties and fathers work with the moms and *kohkums* to keep the kids safe, keep them at home." Sally also stated that "moms and kids need the fathers and aunties. They're like our first line of defence." The third circle is constituted by cousins as well as friends who are "like family," individuals whom anthropologists call "fictive kin" and participants call "heart family." According to Raylynne, "You can always count on cousins, whether they're blood cousins or heart cousins, you can count on them to take you in, to have your back, to have your kid's back, and just be there." The fourth and outer circle includes Elders, grandfathers, and community leaders. "It's like when a kid puts on layers of coats on a cold day," Rachel explained. "The coat closest to you [is] the moms and *kohkums*. The outside coat is, like, the grandfathers and Elders. The aunties and Dads and cousins are the layers in between." She added, "That kid is going to be *real* warm."

This structure of kin-based care was referenced by over 70 per cent of the mothers and fathers with whom I worked. Some participants, like Raylynne and Rachel, described it in considerable detail. Others spoke of it more generally. Regardless of the specificity, however, the majority of research participants described these circles of care and trust as constituting a home that is simultaneously public and private. "I had a teacher who used to say that 'home is where the heart is,'" Raylynne recalled as she described one of the sixteen photographs she took in The 601 (Photo 9). "But in Indian country, home is where the hearts are. In HIV country, our hearts are in our houses with our kids, on the streets, and especially right here in The 601. Our hearts are where our families are. That's where we belong."

Photo 8. Johnny's computer

Photo 9. The 601

The research participants' photographs and descriptions of their extended and public homes paint a very different picture of the community than that described by the moral entrepreneurs who attended the 2012 neighbourhood meeting. The research participants see it as a place where kin-based care and maternal love define it as home. "I know the haters are out there but Hayley and me love our kids," George said slowly as he stared at the photograph of the library. "As long as we got places like this, we got a good home. I don't plan on going no place else." Ironically, this is the same library where the neighbourhood meeting was held a year after George and I spoke. The place that George described as an extension of home, where he feels at his best as a father and where he looks with pride at his children, was where his virtues as a father and Hayley's virtues as a mother were summarily dismissed. In a moment of uncanny prescience, George noted that "there'll be a day when I won't be welcome there. But right now? This is a good place for Hayley and me to put the love."

CONCLUSION

Anne Harrington (2016, 95) claims that "behind every idea of mother love [is] a specter of defective mother love – of mother love gone wrong." AIDS Saskatoon mothers represent that spectre to many. Their neighbourhoods are often sites of hostility and stigma. "They don't *listen* to me when I tell them that I *love* my boys and they love me. And I don't just talk about loving them, I take good care of them and keep them safe," Rachel explained with a sense of incredulity that reminded me of Isabel's confusion when CFS took Mark away from her. "I got my brother and his wife. And my mom and aunties and seven cousins. And we all look after my boys. So how can the people all around here say I don't take care of them?" Rachel continued. "They just don't know where to look to see that we all love my boys."

For almost all the research participants, love is represented by place as well as through words and actions. PWAS at AIDS Saskatoon know very well where to look to find maternal and familial love. Anthropologist Margaret Rodman (1992, 648) would interpret this as evidence that maternal love is autochthonous. It connects people and places through shared cultural histories and experiences that create unique environments of mutual trust and enduring kinship. There is, therefore, much at stake for AIDS Saskatoon mothers in protecting their homes, keeping them intact, and representing them in the best light that they can.

These high stakes may be why the research participants never spoke about domestic violence. This is a significant silence. Josephine Mazonde and Billie Thurston (2013, 211) argue that HIV and domestic violence are syndemically connected in the lives of the Indigenous women with whom they worked in British Columbia: "It was difficult for us to focus on either HIV/AIDS or IPV [intimate partner violence] and not to have the other issue immediately come into the picture." Domestic violence disproportionately victimizes women in all communities, but Indigenous women are particularly vulnerable (Canadian Centre for Justice Statistics 2016). In fact, Indigenous women in Canada are three times more likely to experience violence of all kinds than non-Indigenous women (Brennan 2011, 7). The proportion of Indigenous women among female homicide victims went from 9 per cent in 1980 to 24 per cent in 2015 (Statistics Canada 2017b). The majority of these murders occurred in domestic settings. Between 2004 and 2009, approximately 15 per cent of Indigenous women experienced domestic violence (compared to 7 per cent of non-Indigenous women) and were more likely to sustain serious injuries than others in similar circumstances (Brennan 2011; Downe 2014).

Domestic violence demands individual accountability. There is no question. However, domestic violence is not only a series of interpersonal incidents of gendered aggression and victimization. It is also tied to broader cultural and historical processes and hierarchies. Like the HIV syndemic in Saskatchewan, domestic violence against Indigenous women is tied to the state-sanctioned oppression, displacement, and marginalization of Indigenous Peoples across the country. Phil Lane and colleagues (2003) demonstrate that the gendered abuse of power that occurs within intimate relationships is entangled with the political abuse of power that has characterized the state's relationship with First Nations and Métis Peoples for over a century. Domestic violence, then, is a life-threatening reality for individual women and entire Indigenous communities. Yet, *none* of the thirty women or twenty-three men with whom I worked discussed it.

In their multi-sited ethnography of love, marriage, and HIV, Jennifer Hirsch and colleagues (2009, 3) find that men and women go to great lengths "to create protective silences [in order to] construct marriages that feel privately *and* publicly successful." AIDS Saskatoon mothers and fathers go to similar lengths to remain silent about the domestic violence that would threaten not only their relationships but also their homes and kin-based circles of care. I asked AIDS Saskatoon's former outreach coordinator about this silence. "I hardly ever heard any of the PWAS talk about domestic violence," she noted. "I could see plain evidence of it in about 5 per cent of the women in The 601. And I was really close to a lot of those women, but they just never talked about it. It's like they wanted to convince themselves as much as me that they were safe and doing well even though we all know that they were being hurt." Domestic violence in the lives of AIDS Saskatoon mothers appears to be a well-kept but public secret.

Michael Taussig (1999, 5) defines a public secret as "that which is generally known but that cannot be articulated." He argues that such secrets are essential to everyday life. They mask some aspects of reality so that others can be highlighted. The mothers and fathers who participated in this research work hard to prioritize their children's safety, to maintain essential circles of care and trust, and to reduce the HIV-related harm in their lives. Mothers, in particular, desperately want their expressions of love and the integrity of their homes to be recognized and valued. They therefore keep the public secret, masking any violence they might encounter so as not to draw attention away from what they see as otherwise loving homes. This is not without considerable risk. "If a social worker were to find out that any of the PWAS were getting beaten and they didn't tell [the social worker] about it," AIDS Saskatoon's executive director explained, "they would be called out for lying. It would get ugly fast."

Masking domestic violence also brings an elevated risk to the women victimized by it. They may not seek help because that would entail breaking the silence that they feel protects their children and homes. "I'll take anything that anybody throws at me," Rachel said, hitting her chest with her clenched fist. "As long as I get to keep my boys at home where they're safe and they know I love them, then I'll take anything." Susan described it similarly: "I know most of the mothers and *khokums* here [at The 601]. And there isn't one of us who wouldn't die to protect our kids and homes and our rights to be mothers."

The AIDS Saskatoon mothers who are subjected to domestic violence may very likely turn to those in their circles of care for help. Mitigating domestic violence, like managing HIV, can rarely be tackled alone. Rather than discussing this, however, the research participants spoke in detail about stigma, maternal loss, maternal love, loving homes, and circles of collective care. These are the themes that define HIV-affected motherhood and fatherhood in Saskatchewan. Still, as the research progressed, and the silence around domestic violence became deafening, I wondered to what extent AIDS Saskatoon mothers would be freer to break that silence if their love and commitment to their children, families, communities, and homes were more widely acknowledged and valued.

Although most research participants were not interested in discussing "what if" scenarios, Susan was among those who would if it was a scenario of hope. I asked Susan to imagine what life would be like for AIDS Saskatoon mothers if their maternal roles and rights were more publicly respected and supported, if mothers could speak more openly about the challenges they face without fearing retribution. "It would be a whole lot easier," she responded without hesitation. "I mean, if we didn't have to worry so much about proving that we love our kids and take care of our homes, then we'd have a whole lot more time to be taking care of each other." She thought for a moment or two more and added, "There'd be a lot more singing."

7

Closing

> I cannot conceive of a plan of [health] care that incorporates all the history, all the losses, [but] this is precisely what families try to do for one another every day. They conceive of ways to care for one another in a context where their very relations, and the struggle to maintain the everyday, are at stake. Of course, they often fail, and tragically so. But they keep trying until the very end.
>
> – *Angela Garcia (2010, 203)*

"Eight hundred per cent? HIV went up by 800 per cent? That's huge," Mark said, picking up a report that I had on my desk when he and his grandmother, Isabel, arrived at my office. Mark was almost seventeen years old and a full foot taller than his *kohkum*. He was a starter on his high school football team. The boy I had met almost a decade before was now a young man, and he was thinking about coming to university. "He'll be here year after next," Isabel said with a proud smile. I was struck by how much Mark reminded me of Dennis. The way he queried the HIV rates was reminiscent of Dennis's comments about global HIV/AIDS rates. Mark returned the epidemiological report to my desk: "Wow, that's depressing."

In 2017, rates of HIV/AIDS increased throughout the province. They were up eightfold in the Sunrise Health Region in the east of the province (Soloducha 2018). According to the Saskatchewan Ministry of

Health (2018), almost 80 per cent of those who were newly diagnosed were women of child-bearing age, many of whom already have children. Over 25 per cent of new AIDS cases were diagnosed late in their disease progression, making treatment difficult. Almost half of the people who had been diagnosed with AIDS in the previous ten years had died. Fentanyl and methamphetamine overdoses were at an all-time high. The provincial HIV strategy expired in 2014, limiting the available budget. To make things even worse, health care is a provincial responsibility but First Nations health care falls within a federal portfolio and there is no clear HIV/AIDS-related leadership. HIV-affected communities, particularly the Indigenous communities, were falling between the cracks of the federal and provincial mandates. Globally, almost forty million were living with HIV and five thousand more became infected every day. Mark was absolutely right. It was, and is, depressing.

Despite our talk about the worrisome HIV/AIDS trends, seeing Isabel and Mark was refreshing. I was in the midst of analyzing and writing up the results of the AIDS Saskatoon research. This phase of any project is individual and isolating. It contrasts sharply with the necessarily social and collaborative process of ethnographic fieldwork. In the lonelier post-fieldwork moments, the weight of loss, suffering, and death became overwhelming. It was made worse by the fact that in the previous few years, more PWAS at AIDS Saskatoon had died: Francine, Tyler, Raylynne, Janice, Sally, and Ben.

It is not unusual to read about death in ethnographic texts. Anthropologists often work with communities where structural inequities and hardship lead to early and unexpected passings. The resulting grief and bereavement often draw our attention. The anthropologist's own grief, however, rarely figures into the story. There are many reasons for that. Primary among them is that the story is not about us and – in my view at least – it *should not be about us*. We are also torn, as Jennifer Carroll (2016) so beautifully puts it, between the obligation to conform to standards of sober, analytical anthropological science and the impulse to emotionally eulogize. Grappling with grief, torn obligations, and the isolation of analysis can lead to despair. But the visit with Isabel and Mark was a reminder that the research participants themselves have often and already carved a path forward. Families affected by the HIV/AIDS syndemic in Saskatchewan and around the world maintain a commitment to collective care, to family, and to life.

In his work on the structural violence of HIV/AIDS in Haiti, Paul Farmer (2013, 129) argues that "when the stakes are high, so too must be our standards." He is referring here to the ultimate stakes of survival and health. Standards for health care, political leadership, and global compassion must be high in order to ensure the safety and well-being of those who live amidst infections of inequality. We can reach those standards in the global and local responses to HIV/AIDS syndemics if we centre them on the principles of collective care that are so well represented in Indigenous communities, and the organizations that serve them, worldwide.

The Government of Saskatchewan now provides funds for peer-to-peer support programs for those affected by the HIV/AIDS syndemic. HIV testing is available at more sites and family members are allowed to accompany those getting tested. AIDS Saskatoon has grown to twelve full-time staff. A family support program began in 2015, providing ongoing and emergency assistance of all kinds – housing, child care, recovery support – to entire families. Soul food lunches are now provided every day. An HIV/AIDS hospice that includes prenatal and family-centred services was established in 2015, not far from The 601. There is still much more work to do, but these steps forward are important because they are guided by the strengths, needs, and cultural priorities of many of the same people who contributed to this research.

AIDS Saskatoon is opening the first sanctioned consumption site in the province. Sanctioned consumption sites provide a safe place for supervised substance use. With paramedics on hand, opioid overdoses will be treated immediately and deaths will be reduced. Moreover, a safe consumption site will limit the transmission of HIV and HCV through the provision of clean needles and other prophylaxis. The site is going to serve over three hundred people per day (Vescera 2019). However, to accommodate the safe consumption site, AIDS Saskatoon is relocating once again. The new facility is in a neighbourhood adjacent to where the agency was during this research. The 601 as we know it is shutting its doors.

"What? The 601 is closing?" Mark asked. As we made our way across campus, Isabel and I had been catching up on news from The 601, including its relocation. "Yeah. I sure am going to miss it," Isabel replied. "It was home. The new place will be real different but it will work out. We'll take care of things. After all, it's still a *kikosewin* thing."

References

Acker, Caroline J. 2002. *Creating the American Junkie: Addiction Research in the Classic Era of Narcotic Control*. Baltimore: Johns Hopkins University Press.

Allen, John. 2015. *Home: How Habitat Made Us Human*. New York: Basic Books.

Anderson, E.N. 2011. "Emotions, Motivation, and Behavior in Cognitive Anthropology." In *A Companion to Cognitive Anthropology*, edited by David B. Kronenfeld, Giovanni Bennardo, Victor C. de Munck, and Michael D. Fischer, 314–30. Oxford: Blackwell.

Anderson, Kim. 2000. *A Recognition of Being: Reconstructing Native Womanhood*. Toronto: Sumach.

———. 2003. "Vital Signs: Reading Colonialism in Contemporary Adolescent Family Planning." In *Strong Women Stories: Native Vision and Community Survival*, edited by Kim Anderson and Bonita Lawrence, 173–90. Toronto: Sumach.

———. 2007. "Giving Life to the People: An Indigenous Ideology of Motherhood." In *Maternal Theory: Essential Readings*, edited by Andrea O'Reilly, 761–81. Toronto: Demeter.

Anderson, Kim, and Dawn Memee Lavell-Harvard. 2014. "Growing Up: A Dialogue between Kim Anderson and Dawn Memee Lavell-Harvard on Personal and Professional Evolutions in Indigenous Mothering." In *Mothers of the Nations: Indigenous Mothering as Global Resistance, Reclaiming and Recovery*, edited by D. Memee Lavell-Harvard and Kim Anderson, 291–303. Toronto: Demeter.

Apple, Rima. 2006. *Perfect Motherhood: Science and Childrearing in America*. New Brunswick, NJ: Rutgers University Press.

Arriagada, Paula. 2016. "First Nations, Métis and Inuit Women." In *Women in Canada: A Gender-Based Statistical Report*. Ottawa: Statistics Canada.

https://www150.statcan.gc.ca/n1/en/pub/89-503-x/2015001/article/14313-eng.pdf?st=UPWJ4G_y.

Bagelman, Jen, Fiona Devereaux, and Ravel Hartley. 2016. "Feasting for Change: Reconnection with Food, Place, and Culture." *International Journal of Indigenous Health* 11 (1): 6–17. https://doi.org/10.18357/ijih111201616016.

Ball, Jessica. 2010. "Indigenous Fathers' Involvement in Reconstituting 'Circles of Care.'" *American Journal of Community Psychology* 45: 124–38. https://doi.org/10.1007/s10464-009-9293-1.

Banks, Marcus. 2001. *Visual Methods in Social Research*. London: Sage.

Banwell, Cathy, and Gabriele Bammer. 2006. "Maternal Habits: Narratives of Mothering, Social Position and Drug Use." *International Journal of Drug Policy* 17 (6): 504–13. doi:10.1016/j.drugpo.2006.09.005.

Barnard, Alan. 2002. "Rules and Prohibitions: The Form and Content of Human Kinship." In *Companion Encyclopedia of Anthropology*, edited by Tim Ingold, 783–812. London: Routledge.

Baskin, Cyndy, and Bela McPherson. 2014. "Towards the Wellbeing of Aboriginal Mothers and Their Families." In *Mothers of the Nations: Indigenous Mothering as Global Resistance, Reclaiming and Recovery*, edited by D. Memee Lavell-Harvard and Kim Anderson, 109–29. Toronto: Demeter.

Beatty, Andrew. 2014. "Anthropology and Emotion." *Journal of the Royal Anthropological Institute* 20 (3): 545–63. https://doi.org/10.1111/1467-9655.12114.

Beck, Julie. 2011. "FYI: Can a Woman Really Lift a Car Off Her Pinned Child?" *Popular Science*, August 11, 2011. http://www.popsci.com/science/article/2011-07/fyi-can-woman-really-lift-car-her-pinned-child.

Becker, Howard S. 1963. *Outsiders: Studies in the Sociology of Deviance*. New York: Free Press.

Bedor, Emma, and Atsushi Tajima. 2012. "No Fat Moms! Celebrity Mothers' Weight Loss Narratives in *People* Magazine." *Journal of Magazine and New Media Research* 13 (2): 1–26. https://pdfs.semanticscholar.org/8d38/1f714dd1ff65dd9272aff4f10ad7125d4da7.pdf?_ga=2.57133039.478811338.1591894348-938542574.1591894348.

Beegle, Kathleen, Joachim DeWeerdt, and Stefan Dercon. 2009. "The Intergenerational Impact of the African Orphan Crisis: A Cohort Study from an HIV/AIDS Affected Area." *International Journal of Epidemiology* 38 (2): 561–8. https://doi.org/10.1093/ije/dyn197.

Bekoff, Marc. 2011. "Grief, Mourning, and Broken-Hearted Animals." *Psychology Today*, November 26, 2011. https://www.psychologytoday.com/blog/animal-emotions/201111/grief-mourning-and-broken-hearted-animals.

Benkwitz, Adam. 2016. "Brief Encounters with Qualitative Methods in Health Research: Ethnography." *Cumbria Partnership Journal of Research,*

Practice, and Learning 5 (1): 3–7. https://pdfs.semanticscholar.org/6102/d2b593e194e4ef3b5b48f442baf96e7bc67b.pdf?_ga=2.253578444.478811338.1591894348-938542574.1591894348.

Block, Ellen, and Will McGrath. 2019. *Infected Kin: Orphan Care and AIDS in Lesotho*. New Brunswick, NJ: Rutgers University Press.

Bogin, Barry. 1997. "Evolutionary Hypotheses for Human Childhood." *Yearbook of Physical Anthropology* 40: 63–89. https://onlinelibrary.wiley.com/doi/pdf/10.1002/%28SICI%291096-8644%281997%2925%2B%3C63%3A%3AAID-AJPA3%3E3.0.CO%3B2-8.

Bourgois, Philippe. 2003. *In Search of Respect: Selling Crack in El Barrio*. 2nd ed. Cambridge: University of Cambridge Press.

Boyd, Susan. 1999. *Mothers and Illicit Drugs: Transcending the Myths*. Toronto: University of Toronto Press.

Bramlett, Matthew, and Stephen Blumberg. 2007. "Family Structure and Children's Physical and Mental Health." *Health Affairs* 26 (2): 549–58. https://doi.org/10.1377/hlthaff.26.2.549.

Brant, Jennifer. 2014. "Aboriginal Mothering: Honouring the Past, Nurturing the Future." In *Mothers, Mothering, and Motherhood across Cultural Differences*, edited by Andrea O'Reilly, 7–40. Toronto: Demeter.

Brennan, Shannon. 2011. *Violent Victimization of Aboriginal Women in Canadian Provinces*. Ottawa: Statistics Canada.

Brewer, Athena. 2016. "How Do I Tell My Kids I Have HIV?" *The Advocate*, December 16, 2016. http://www.hivplusmag.com/just-diagnosed/2016/5/05/how-do-i-tell-my-kids-i-have-hiv.

Bristow, Jennie. 2013. "Reporting the Riots: Parenting Culture and the Problem of Authority in Media Analysis of August 2011." *Sociological Review Online* 18 (4): 100–10. https://doi.org/10.5153%2Fsro.3147.

Bulloch, Andrew, Jeanne Williams, Dina Lavorato, and Scott Patten. 2016. "Trends in Binge Drinking in Canada from 1996 to 2013: A Repeated Cross-Sectional Analysis." *Canadian Medical Association Journal Open* 4(4): E599–E604. https://doi.org/10.9778/cmajo.20150124.

Campbell, Nancy. 2000. *Using Women: Gender, Drug Policy, and Social Justice*. New York: Routledge.

Canadian Centre for Justice Statistics. 2016. *Family Violence in Canada: A Statistical Profile, 2014*. Ottawa: Statistics Canada.

Canadian Institutes for Health Research. 2019. *Opioid Prescribing in Canada: How Are Practices Changing?* Ottawa: Canadian Institutes for Health Research. https://www.cihi.ca/sites/default/files/document/opioid-prescribing-canada-trends-en-web.pdf.

Canadian Women's Foundation. 2014. *The Facts about Women's Poverty*. http://www.canadianwomen.org/facts-about-women-and-poverty.

Cantisano, Nicole, Bernard Rimé, and Maria Teresa Munoz Sastre. 2015. "The Importance of Quality over Quantity in the Social Sharing of Emotion (SSE) in People Living with HIV/AIDS." *Psychology, Health, and Medicine* 20 (1): 103–13. https://doi.org/10.1080/13548506.2014.901544.

Caplan, Paula. 2007. "Don't Blame Mother: Then and Now." In *Maternal Theory: Essential Readings*, edited by Andrea O'Reilly, 592–600. Toronto: Demeter.

Carroll, Jennifer J. 2016. "Writing Grief: Death and Bereavement in Ethnographic Texts." *Medical Anthropology Theory*, May 30. http://www.medanthrotheory.org/read/6231/writing-grief.

Carsten, Janet. 1995. "The Substance of Kinship and the Heat of the Hearth: Feeding, Personhood, and Relatedness among Malays in Pulua Langkawi." *American Ethnologist* 22 (2): 223–41. https://doi.org/10.1525/ae.1995.22.2.02a00010.

———, ed. 2000. *Cultures of Relatedness: New Approaches to the Study of Kinship*. Cambridge: Cambridge University Press.

———. 2004. *After Kinship*. Cambridge: Cambridge University Press.

CBC News. 2015. "'No Natives Please': Kijiji Pulls Apartment Ad for Prince Albert, Sask. after Complaint." August 25, 2015. http://www.cbc.ca/news/canada/saskatoon/no-natives-please-kijiji-pulls-apartment-ad-for-prince-albert-sask-after-complaint-1.3202505.

———. 2019. "Regina, Saskatoon Have Some of the Highest Crime Severity Numbers in the Country." July 22, 2019. https://www.cbc.ca/news/canada/saskatoon/regina-saskatoon-crime-severity-rates-1.5220235.

Chainey, Naomi. 2017. "Our Disturbing Impulse to Blame the Charlottesville Driver's Mother for His Actions." *Sydney Morning Herald*, August 17, 2017. http://www.smh.com.au/lifestyle/news-and-views/opinion/our-disturbing-impulse-to-blame-the-charlottesville-drivers-mother-for-his-actions-20170816-gxxoxp.html.

Charbonneau, Sinéad, Robina Thomas, Aitlin Janzen, Jeannine Carrière, Susan Strega, and Leslie Brown. 2014. "Storying the Untold: Indigenous Motherhood and Street Sex Work." In *Mothers of the Nations: Indigenous Mothering as Global Resistance, Reclaiming and Recovery*, edited by D. Memee Lavell-Harvard and Kim Anderson, 163–78. Toronto: Demeter.

Chua, Amy. 2011. *Battle Hymn of the Tiger Mother*. New York: Penguin.

Clemenson, Nana. 2016. "Exploring Ambiguous Realms: Access, Exposure, and Agency in the Interactions of Rural Zambian Children." *Childhood* 23 (3): 317–32. https://doi.org/10.1177%2F0907568216633509.

Clinton, Hillary Rodham. 1996. *It Takes a Village: And Other Lessons Children Teach Us*. New York: Simon and Schuster.

Coertze, Bronwyne, Ashraf Kagee, and Ruth Bland. 2015. "Barriers and Facilitators to Paediatric Adherence to Antiretroviral Therapy in Rural South Africa: A Multi-stakeholder Perspective." *AIDS Care* 27 (3): 315–21. doi: 10.1080/09540121.2014.967658.

Colten, Mary Ellen. 1982. "Attitudes, Experiences, and Self Perceptions of Heroin Addicted Mothers." *Journal of Social Issues* 38 (2): 77–92. https://doi.org/10.1111/j.1540-4560.1982.tb00119.x.

Connolly, Deborah. 2000. "Mythical Mothers and Dichotomies of Good and Evil: Homeless Mothers in the United States." In *Ideologies and Technologies of Motherhood: Race, Class, Sexuality, Nationalism*, edited by Heléna Ragoné and France Winddance Twine, 263–94. New York: Routledge.

Conway, Brian, Jason Grebley, Harout Tosconian, Dennis Lefebvre, and Stanley deVlaming. 2005. "A Systematic Approach to the Treatment of HIV and Hepatitis C Virus Infection in the Inner City: A Canadian Perspective." *Clinical Infectious Disease* 41 (1): 73–8. https://doi.org/10.1086/429500.

Corrado, Raymond R., Sarah Kuehn, and Irna Margaritescu. 2014. "Policy Issues Regarding the Overrepresentation of Incarcerated Aboriginal Offenders in a Canadian Context." *Youth Justice* 14 (1): 40–62. https://doi.org/10.1177%2F1473225413520361.

Crocq, Marc-Antoine. 2007. "Historical and Cultural Aspects of Man's Relationship with Addictive Drugs." *Dialogues in Clinical Neuroscience* 9 (4): 355–61. https://www.ncbi.nlm.nih.gov/pmc/articles/PMC3202501/.

Crowe, Cathy. 2007. *Dying for a Home: Homeless Activists Speak Out*. Toronto: Between the Lines.

Cull, Randi. 2006. "Aboriginal Mothering under the State's Gaze." In *"Until Our Hearts Are on the Ground": Aboriginal Mothering, Oppression, Resistance and Rebirth*, edited by D. Memee Lavell-Harvard and Jeannette Corbiere Lavell, 141–56. Toronto: Demeter.

Currie, Janet C. 2004. "Manufacturing Addiction: The Overprescription of Tranquilizers and Sleeping Pills to Women in Canada." *Canadian Women's Health Network* 6/7 (4/1). http://www.cwhn.ca/en/node/39526.

Daschuk, James. 2013. *Clearing the Plains: Disease, Politics of Starvation, and the Loss of Aboriginal Life*. Regina: University of Regina Press.

DeBeck, Kora, Evan Wood, Thomas Kerr, and Julio Montaner. 2007. "Harper's New Anti-Drug Strategy is not Anti-HIV." *National Review of Medicine* 4 (15). http://www.mapinc.org/drugnews/v07/n1068/a01.html?7551.

Dégh, Linda, and Andrew Vázsonyi. 1983. "Does the Word 'Dog' Bite? Ostensive Action: A Means of Legend Telling." *Journal of Folklore Research* 20: 5–34.

Demo, Anne Teresa. 2015. "Reframing Motherhood: Factoring in Consumption and Privilege." In *The Motherhood Business: Consumption, Communication, and Privilege*, edited by Anna T. Demo, Jennifer L. Bordo, and Charlotte Kroløkke, 1–27. Tuscaloosa: University of Alabama Press.

Dermott, Esther. 2008. *Intimate Fatherhood: A Sociological Analysis*. London: Routledge.

Dominguez, Virginia. 2016. "Ethics, Work, and Life – Individual Struggles and Professional 'Comfort Zones' in Anthropology." In *Anthropological Ethics in Context: An Ongoing Dialogue*, edited by Dena Plemmons and Alex W. Barkers, 9–21. Walnut Creek, CA: Left Coast Press.

Doucet, Andrea. 2007. *Do Men Mother?* Toronto: University of Toronto Press.

Douglas, Susan J., and Meredith W. Michaels. 2004. *The Mommy Myth: The Idealization of Motherhood and How It Has Undermined All Women*. New York: Free Press.

Downe, Pamela. 2014. "Intersecting Sites of Violence in the Lives of Aboriginal Girls." In *Faces of Violence in the Lives of Girls*, edited by Helene Berman and Yasmin Jiwani, 25–40. London, ON: Althouse.

Downe, Pamela, Britt Agrey, Adriana Appleton, Courtney Black, Gillian Cattet, Marissa Evans, Sheena Fineday, et al. (2016). *AIDS Saskatoon: A Timeline, 1982–2014*. Saskatoon: AnthroInSight.

Dyck, Darryl. 2017. "How a Little Known Patent Sparked Canada's Opioid Crisis." *Globe and Mail*, February 10, 2017. http://www.theglobeandmail.com/news/investigations/oxycontin/article33448409/.

Edwards, Kyle. 2018. "Fighting Foster Care." *Maclean's*, January 9, 2018. https://www.macleans.ca/first-nations-fighting-foster-care/.

Ehrenreich, Barbara, and Dierdre English. 1979. *For Her Own Good: 150 Years of the Experts' Advice to Women*. London: Pluto.

Ehrmann, Tanya. 2002. "Community-Based Organizations and HIV Prevention for Incarcerated Populations: Three HIV Prevention Models." *AIDS Education and Prevention* 14 (5): 75–84. https://doi.org/10.1521/aeap.14.7.75.23866.

Ekman, Paul. 2007. *Emotions Revealed: Recognizing Faces and Feelings to Improve Communication and Emotional Life*. 2nd ed. New York: Holt.

Environment Canada. 2011. *National Climate Data and Information Archive*. https://web.archive.org/web/20120118210015/http://climate.weatheroffice.gc.ca/Welcome_e.html.

Esnard, Talia. 2015. "'We Want to Consistently Address Their Needs': Explorations of the Perceptions, Experiences and Challenges of Parenting Interventions for Incarcerated Mothers." In *The Mother-Blame Game*, edited by Vanessa Reimer and Sarah Sahagian, 136–59. Toronto: Demeter.

Farmer, Paul. 2004. *Pathologies of Power: Health, Human Rights, and the New War on the Poor*. Berkeley: University of California Press.

———. 2013. "Global Health Equity and the Missing Weapons of Mass Salvation." In *To Repair the World: Paul Farmer Speaks to the Next Generation*, edited by Jonathon Weigel, 128–42. Berkeley: University of California Press.

Fawcett, R. Ben, Ryan Walker, and Jonathan Greene. 2015. "Indigenizing City Planning Processes in Saskatoon, Canada." *Canadian Journal of Urban Research* 24 (2): 158–75.

Fiske, Jo-Anne. 1996. "The Womb Is to the Nation as the Heart Is to the Body: Ethnopolitical Discourses of the Canadian Indigenous Women's

Movement." *Studies in Political Economy* 51: 65–95. https://doi.org/10.1080/19187033.1996.11675329.

Furedi, Frank. 2002. *Paranoid Parenting: Why Ignoring the Experts May Be the Best for Your Child*. Chicago: Chicago Review Press.

Gahlinger, Paul. 2001. *Illegal Drugs: A Complete Guide to Their History, Chemistry, Use, and Abuse*. Salt Lake City: Sagebrush.

Galbally, Megan, Andrew Lewis, Marinus Van Ijzendorn, and Michael Permezal. 2011. "The Role of Oxytocin in Mother-Infant Relations: A Systematic Review of Human Studies." *Harvard Review of Psychiatry* 19 (1): 1–14. https://www.researchgate.net/deref/http%3A%2F%2Fdx.doi.org%2F10.3109%2F10673229.2011.549771.

Garcia, Angela. 2010. *The Pastoral Clinic: Addiction and the Dispossession along the Rio Grande*. Berkeley: University of California Press.

Gaskins, Suzanne. 2003. "From Corn to Cash: Change and Continuity within Mayan Families." *Ethos* 31 (2): 248–73. https://doi.org/10.1525/eth.2003.31.2.248.

Gatrell, Caroline. 2011. "Policy and the Pregnant Body at Work: Strategies of Secrecy, Silence and Supra-Performance." *Gender, Work, and Organization* 18 (2): 158–81. https://doi.org/10.1111/j.1468-0432.2009.00485.x.

Gaudry, Adam. 2009. "Métis." In *The Canadian Encyclopedia, Historica Canada*. Last edited September 11, 2019. https://www.thecanadianencyclopedia.ca/en/article/metis.

George, Jane. 2006. "Polar Bear No Match for Fearsome Mother in Ivujivik." *Nunatsiaq News*, February 17, 2006. http://www.nunatsiaqonline.ca/archives/60217/news/nunavut/60217_03.html.

Gibson, Margaret. 2014. "Queer Mothering and the Question of Normalcy." In *Mothers, Mothering, and Motherhood across Cultural Differences*, edited by Andrea O'Reilly, 347–66. Toronto: Demeter.

Goffman, Erving. 1963. *Stigma: Notes on the Management of Spoiled Identities*. New York: Simon and Schuster.

Goldstein, Diane E. 2004. *Once Upon a Virus: AIDS Legends and Vernacular Risk Perception*. Logan: University of Utah Press.

Gore, Ariel. 2007. "High Risk: Who a Mother Should Be." In *Maternal Theory: Essential Readings*, edited by Andrea O'Reilly, 756–60. Toronto: Demeter.

Gosselin, Cheryl. 2006. "'They Let Their Kids Run Wild': The Policing of Aboriginal Mothers in Quebec." In *"Until Our Hearts Are on the Ground": Aboriginal Mothering, Oppression, Resistance and Rebirth*, edited by D. Memee Lavell-Harvard and Jeannette Corbiere Lavell, 196–206. Toronto: Demeter.

Government of Saskatchewan. 2014. *Saskatchewan Child Abuse Protocol*. Regina: Ministry of Social Services.

Guerrina, Roberta. 2014. "Working Mothers: Performing Economic and Gender Identities." In *Mothers, Mothering, and Motherhood across Cultural Differences*, edited by Andrea O'Reilly, 467–86. Toronto: Demeter.

Hackett, Paul. 2005. "Historical Mourning Practices Observed among the Cree and Ojibway Indians of the Central Subarctic." *Ethnohistory* 52 (3): 503–32. https://doi.org/10.1215/00141801-52-3-503.

Hanvey, Louise, and Denise Avard. 1994. *The Health of Canada's Children: A CICH Profile.* Ottawa: Canadian Institute of Child Health.

Hardyment, Christina. 1995. *Perfect Parents: Baby-Care Advice Past and Present.* Oxford: Oxford University Press.

———. 2008. *Dream Babies: Childcare Advice from John Locke to Gina Ford.* London: Francis Lincoln.

Harkness, Sara, and Charles M. Super. 1991. "East Africa." In *Children in Historical and Comparative Perspective*, edited by Joseph M. Hawes and N. Ray Hiner, 217–39. Westport, CT: Greenwood.

Harrington, Anne. 2016. "Mother Love and Mental Illness: An Emotional History." *Osiris* 31: 94–115. https://doi.org/10.1086/687559.

Hawkes, Kristen, J.F. O'Connell, and N.G. Blurton Jones. 1995. "Hadza Children's Foraging: Juvenile Dependency, Social Arrangements, and Mobility among Hunter-Gatherers." *Current Anthropology* 36 (4): 688–700. https://doi.org/10.1086/204420.

Hays, Sharon. 1996. *The Cultural Contradictions of Motherhood.* New Haven, CT: Yale University Press.

———. 2007. "Why Can't a Mother Be More Like a Businessman?" In *Maternal Theory: Essential Readings*, edited by Andrea O'Reilly, 408–30. Toronto: Demeter.

Herie, Marilyn, and Wayne Skinner. 2010. *Substance Abuse in Canada.* Oxford: Oxford University Press.

Hewlett, Barry S. 1991. *Intimate Fathers: The Nature and Context of Aka Pygmy Paternal Infant Care.* Ann Arbor: University of Michigan Press.

———. 2001. "The Cultural Nexus of Father-Infant Bonding." In *Gender in Cross-Cultural Perspective*, edited by Caroline B. Brettell and Carolyn F. Sargent, 45–56. Cambridge: Cambridge University Press.

Heywood, Colin. 2013. "The Child and the Home: A Historical Survey." *Home Cultures* 10 (3): 227–44. https://doi.org/10.2752/175174213X13739735973499.

Hilton, B. Ann, Ray Thompson, Laura Moore-Dempsey, and Randy Janzen. 2001. "Harm Reduction Theories and Strategies for Control of Human Immunodeficiency Virus: A Review of the Literature." *Journal of Advanced Nursing* 33 (3): 357–70. https://doi.org/10.1046/j.1365-2648.2001.01672.x.

Hinton, Denise, Louise Laverty, and Jude Robinson. 2013. "Negotiating (Un)healthy Lifestyles in an Era of Intensive Parenting: Ethnographic Case Studies from North-West England, UK." In *Parenting in Global Perspective: Ideologies of Kinship, Self, and Politics*, edited by Charlotte Faircloth, Diane Hoffman, and Linda Layne, 71–85. London: Routledge.

Hirsch, Jennifer, Holly Wardlow, Daniel Smith, Harriet Phinney, Shanti Parikh, and Constance Nathanson. 2009. *The Secret: Love, Marriage, and HIV.* Nashville: Vanderbilt University Press.

Holmes, J. Teresa. 2009. "When Blood Matters: Making Kinship in Colonial Kenya." In *Kinship and Beyond: The Genealogical Model Reconsidered*, edited by Sandra Bamford and James Leach, 50–83. London: Berghahn Books.

Hrvatin, Vanessa. 2019. "Motherhood's Last Taboo." *Saskatoon Star Phoenix*, April 27, 2019, NP2–3.

Hunleth, Jean. 2013. "Children's Roles in Tuberculosis Treatment Regimes: Constructing Childhood and Kinship in Urban Zambia." *Medical Anthropology Quarterly* 27 (2): 292–311. https://dx.doi.org/10.1111%2Fmaq.12028.

———. 2017. *Children as Caregivers: The Global Fight against Tuberculosis and HIV in Zambia*. New Brunswick, NJ: Rutgers University Press.

Hymowitz, Kay. 2003. "Bringing Up Parents." *Commentary*, June 2003, 50–3. https://www.commentarymagazine.com/articles/kay-hymowitz/bringing-up-parents/.

Iliffe, John. 2006. *The African AIDS Epidemic: A History*. Athens: Ohio University Press.

Ing, Rosalyn. 2006. "Canada's Indian Residential Schools and Their Impacts on Mothering." In *"Until Our Hearts Are on the Ground": Aboriginal Mothering, Oppression, Resistance and Rebirth*, edited by D. Memee Lavell-Harvard and Jeannette Corbiere Lavell, 157–72. Toronto: Demeter.

Ingram, Alan. 2008. "Domopolitics and Disease: HIV/AIDS, Immigration and Asylum in the UK." *Environment and Planning* 26 (5): 875–94. https://doi.org/10.1068%2Fd2208.

Innes, Robert A. 2010. "Elder Brother, the Law of the People, and Contemporary Kinship Practices of Cowessess First Nation Members: Reconceptualizing Kinship in American Indian Studies Research." *American Indian Culture and Research Journal* 34 (2): 27–46. https://doi.org/10.17953/aicr.34.2.y0x7k043337k7w03.

Jankowiak, William. 2011. "The Han Chinese Family: The Realignment of Parenting Ideals, Sentiments, and Practices." In *Women and Gender in Contemporary Chinese Societies: Beyond Han Patriarchy*, edited by Shanshan Du and Yah-Chen Chen, 109–32. Lanham, MD: Lexington.

Jarrett, Robin L., Stephanie R. Jefferson, and Jenell Kelly. 2010. "Finding Community in Family: Neighborhood Effects and African American Kin Networks." *Journal of Comparative Family Studies* 41 (3): 299–328. https://doi.org/10.3138/jcfs.41.3.299.

Jenks, Elaine Bass. 2005. "Explaining Disability: Parents' Stories of Raising Children with Visual Impairments in a Sighted World." *Journal of Contemporary Ethnography* 34 (2): 143–69. https://doi.org/10.1177%2F0891241604272064.

Johnston, Patrick. 1983. *Native Children and the Child Welfare System*. Toronto: Canadian Council on Social Development.

Jürgens, Ralf, Jonathon Cohen, Edwin Cameron, Scott Buris, Michaela Clayton, Richard Elliott, Richard Pearshouse, et al. 2009. "Ten Reasons to Oppose the Criminalization of HIV Exposure or Transmission." *Reproductive Health Matters* 17 (3/4): 163–72. https://doi.org/10.1016/S0968-8080(09)34462-6.

Kanner, Leo. 1973. *Childhood Psychoses: Initial Studies and New Insights*. New York: John Wiley and Sons.

Kaptan, Senem. 2011. "Navigating the Tricky Waters of Maternal Militarization: Experiences of Being a Soldier's Mother in Turkey." In *An Anthropology of Mothering*, edited by Michelle Walks and Naomi MacPherson, 253–65. Toronto: Demeter.

Kidman, Rachel, and Tia Palermo. 2016. "The Relationship between Parental Presence and Child Sexual Violence: Evidence from Thirteen Countries in Sub-Saharan Africa." *Child Abuse and Neglect* 51: 172–80. https://doi.org/10.1016/j.chiabu.2015.10.018.

King, Thomas. 2013. *The Inconvenient Indian: A Curious Account of Native People in North America*. Toronto: Anchor Canada.

Knight, Kelly Ray. 2015. *Addicted, Pregnant, Poor*. Durham, NC: Duke University Press.

Kolahdooz, Fariba, Fouz Nader, Kyoung Yi, and Sangita Sharma. 2015. "Understanding the Social Determinants of Health among Indigenous Canadians: Priorities for Health Promotion, Policies, and Actions." *Global Health Action* 8: 1–16. https://doi.org/10.3402/gha.v8.27968.

Krampe, Edythe, and Paul D. Fairweather. 1993. "Father Presence and Father Formation: A Theoretical Reformulation." *Journal of Family Issues* 14 (4): 573–93. https://doi.org/10.1177%2F019251393014004006.

Kristeva, Julia. 1982. *Powers of Horror: An Essay on Abjection*. New York: Columbia University Press.

Ladd-Taylor, Molly. 2007. "Mother-Worship/Mother-Blame: Politics and Welfare in an Uncertain Age." In *Maternal Theory: Essential Readings*, edited by Andrea O'Reilly, 660–7. Toronto: Demeter.

LaFromboise, Teresa, Joseph E. Trimble, and Gerald V. Mohatt. 1990. "Counseling Interventions and American Indian Tradition: An Integrative Approach." *Counseling Psychologist* 18 (4): 628–54. https://doi.org/10.1177%2F0011000090184006.

Lamb, Michael E. 2000. "The History of Research on Father Involvement." *Marriage and Family Review* 29 (2/3): 23–42. https://doi.org/10.1300/J002v29n02_03.

Lancy, David. 2015. *The Anthropology of Childhood: Cherubs, Chattel, Changlings*. 2nd ed. Cambridge: University of Cambridge Press.

Lane, Phil, Julie Bopp, and Michael Bopp. 2003. *Aboriginal Domestic Violence in Canada*. Ottawa: Aboriginal Healing Foundation.

Lareau, Annette. 2011. *Unequal Childhoods: Class, Race, and Family Life*. 2nd ed. Berkeley: University of California Press.

LaRossa, Ralph. 1997. *The Modernization of Fatherhood: A Social and Political History*. Chicago: University of Chicago Press.

Lavell-Harvard, D. Memee, and Kim Anderson. 2014. "Indigenous Mothering Perspectives." In *Mothers of the Nations: Indigenous Mothering as Global Resistance, Reclaiming and Recovery*, edited by D. Memee Lavell-Harvard and Kim Anderson, 1–11. Toronto: Demeter.

Lavell-Harvard, D. Memee, and Jeannette Corbiere Lavell. 2006. "Aboriginal Women vs. Canada: The Struggle for Our Mothers to Remain Aboriginal." In *"Until Our Hearts Are on the Ground": Aboriginal Mothering, Oppression, Resistance and Rebirth*, edited by D. Memee Lavell-Harvard and Jeannette Corbiere Lavell, 184–95. Toronto: Demeter.

Lee, Ellie, Jennie Bristow, Charlotte Faircloth, and Jan Macvarish. 2014. *Parenting Culture Studies*. New York: Palgrave Macmillan.

Lee, Ellie, Jan Macvarish, and Jennie Bristow. 2010. "Risk, Health, and Parenting Culture." *Health, Risk, and Society* 12 (4): 293–300. https://doi.org/10.1080/13698571003789732.

Leo, Geoff. 2015. "HIV Rates on Saskatchewan Reserves Higher than Some African Nations." *CBC News*, June 30, 2015. https://www.cbc.ca/news/canada/saskatchewan/hiv-rates-on-sask-reserves-higher-than-some-african-nations-1.3097231.

Levine, Susan. 2003. "Documentary Film and HIV/AIDS: New Directions for Applied Visual Anthropology in Southern Africa." *Visual Anthropology Review* 19 (1/2): 57–72. https://doi.org/10.1525/var.2003.19.1-2.57.

Link, Bruce, and Jo C. Phelan. 2001. "Conceptualizing Stigma." *Annual Review of Sociology* 27 (1): 363–85. https://doi.org/10.1146/annurev.soc.27.1.363.

LivingMyCulture. 2016. "Indigenous Voices: Honouring Our Loss and Grief." Video presentation. http://livingmyculture.ca/culture/first-nations/indigenous-voices-honouring-our-loss-and-grief/?topic=After+Death+and+Ceremonies. Accessed July 11, 2017.

Lockwood, Penelope, and Ziva Kunda. 1997. "Superstars and Me: Predicting the Impact of Role Models on the Self." *Journal of Personality and Social Psychology* 73 (1): 91–103. https://psycnet.apa.org/doi/10.1037/0022-3514.73.1.91.

Lupton, Deborah. 2011. "'The Best Thing for the Baby': Mothers' Concepts and Experiences Related to Promoting their Infants' Health and Development." *Health, Risk, and Society* 13 (7/8): 637–51. https://doi.org/10.1080/13698575.2011.624179.

Lutz, Catherine. 1998. *Unnatural Emotions: Everyday Sentiments on a Micronesian Atoll and Their Challenge to Western Thought*. 2nd ed. Chicago: University of Chicago Press.

Lutz, Catherine, and Geoffrey White. 1986. "The Anthropology of Emotions." *Annual Review of Anthropology* 15: 405–36. https://doi.org/10.1146/annurev.an.15.100186.002201.

Lux, Maureen. 2001. *Medicine That Walks: Disease, Medicine, and Canadian Plains Native People, 1880–1940*. Toronto: University of Toronto Press.

MacQueen, Ken. 2015. "Saskatchewan's HIV Epidemic: Third World Levels of HIV Infection Rates in One of the World's Wealthiest Countries Are a National Disgrace." *Maclean's*, July 22, 2015. https://www.macleans.ca/news/canada/saskatchewans-hiv-epidemic/.

Malinowski, Bronislaw. 1929. *The Sexual Life of Savages: An Ethnographic Account of Courtship, Marriage, and Family Life among the Natives of the Trobriand Islands*. London: Routledge, Kegan and Paul.

Marcotta, Marsha. 2009. "Relentless Rebuke: 'Experts' and the Scripting of 'Good' Mothers." In *Mother Knows Best: Talking Back to the "Experts,"* edited by Jessica Nathanson and Laura C. Tuley, 203–12. Toronto: Demeter.

Martin, Bianca, Mariela Mitre, James D'amour, Moses Chao, and Robert Froemke. 2015. "Oxytocin Enables Maternal Behavior by Balancing Corticol Inhibition." *Nature* 520: 499–504. https://doi.org/10.1038/nature14402.

Martin, Wednesday. 2015. *Primates of Park Avenue*. New York: Simon and Schuster.

Mashegone, S., and N.F. Mohale. 2016. "Parenting AIDS-Orphaned Grandchildren: Experiences from Lephale, South Africa." *Gender and Behavior* 14 (1): 6931–43. https://www.ajol.info/index.php/gab/article/view/143502.

Mayan, Maria. 2009. *Essentials of Qualitative Inquiry*. Walnut Creek, CA: Left Coast Press.

Mazonde, Josephine, and Wilfreda (Billie) Thurston. 2013. "HIV Is My 'Best' Problem: Living with Racism, HIV, and Interpersonal Violence." In *Women, Motherhood, and Living with HIV/AIDS: A Cross-Cultural Perspective*, edited by Pranee Liamputtong, 201–14. New York: Springer.

McEvoy, Maureen, and Judith Daniluk. 1995. "Wounds of the Soul: The Experience of Aboriginal Women Survivors of Sexual Abuse." *Canadian Psychology* 36 (3): 221–35.

Mead, Margaret. 1935. *Sex and Temperament in Three Primitive Societies*. New York: Harper Collins.

———. 1938. *The Mountain Arapesh*. Washington, DC: American Museum of Natural History.

Milan, Anne, Leslie-Anne Keown, and Covadonga Robles Urquijo. 2015. "Families, Living Arrangements, and Unpaid Work." In *Women in Canada: A Gender-Based Statistical Report*. http://www.statcan.gc.ca/pub/89-503-x/2010001/article/11546-eng.htm.

Miller, Jim. 1996. *Shingwauk's Vision: A History of Native Residential Schools*. Toronto: University of Toronto Press.

Miller, Lisa. 2010. "The Bear Truth: Will the 'Mama Grizzlies' Really Protect America's Kids?" *News Week*, October 4, 2010. https://www.newsweek.com/what-does-mama-grizzly-really-mean-72001.

Moore, Danièle, and Margaret Macdonald. 2013. "Language and Literary Development in a Canadian Native Community: Halq'eméylem

Revitalization in Stó:lō Head Start Program in British Columbia." *Modern Language Journal* 97 (3): 702–19. https://doi.org/10.1111/j.1540-4781.2013.12028.x.

Mullings, Leith. 2005. "Resistance and Resilience: The Sojourner Syndrome and the Social Context of Reproduction in Central Harlem." *Transforming Anthropology* 13 (2): 79–91. https://doi.org/10.1525/tran.2005.13.2.79.

Murphy, Debra A., Erika F. Austin, and Lisa Greenwell. 2006. "Correlates of HIV-Related Stigma among HIV-Positive Mothers and Their Uninfected Adolescent Children." *Women & Health* 44 (3): 19–42. https://doi.org/10.1300/J013v44n03_02.

National Collaborating Centre for Aboriginal Health (NCCAH). 2013. *The Sacred Space of Womanhood: Mothering across Generations*. Prince George, BC: National Collaborating Centre for Aboriginal Health.

National Inquiry into Missing and Murdered Indigenous Women and Girls. 2019. "Reclaiming Power and Place: Executive Summary of the Final Report of the National Inquiry into Missing and Murdered Indigenous Women and Girls." https://www.mmiwg-ffada.ca/wp-content/uploads/2019/06/Executive_Summary.pdf.

Neumann, Inga. 2007. "Oxytocin: The Neuropeptide of Love Reveals Some of Its Secrets." *Cell Metabolism* 5 (4): 231–3. https://doi.org/10.1016/j.cmet.2007.03.008.

Ng, Irene, Rosemary Sarri, and Elizabeth Stoffregen. 2013. "Intergenerational Incarceration: Risk Factors and Social Exclusion." *Journal of Poverty* 17 (4): 437–59. https://doi.org/10.1080/10875549.2013.833161.

Nielson, Linda. 1999. "Stepmothers: Why So Much Stress? A Review of the Literature." *Journal of Divorce and Remarriage* 30 (1/2): 115–48. https://doi.org/10.1300/J087v30n01_08.

Nussbaum, Martha. 2001. *Upheavals of Thought: The Intelligence of Emotions*. Cambridge: Cambridge University Press.

Nyamukapa, Constance, and Simon Gregson. 2005. "Extended Family's and Women's Roles in Safeguarding Orphans' Education in AIDS-Afflicted Rural Zimbabwe." *Social Science and Medicine* 60 (10): 2155–67. https://doi.org/10.1016/j.socscimed.2004.10.005.

O'Donnell, Vivian, and Susan Wallace. 2015. "First Nations, Metis and Inuit Women." In *Women in Canada: A Gender-Based Statistical Report*. https://www150.statcan.gc.ca/n1/pub/89-503-x/2010001/article/11442-eng.htm.

Olsen, Anna, Cathy Banwell, and Annie Madden. 2014. "Contraception, Punishment, and Women Who Use Drugs." *BMC Women's Health* 14 (5). https://doi.org/10.1186/1472-6874-14-5.

Office of the Correctional Investigator, Government of Canada. 2013. "Aboriginal Offenders: A Critical Situation." http://www.oci-bec.gc.ca/cnt/rpt/oth-aut/oth-aut20121022info-eng.aspx.

Olynick, Janna, Han Z. Li, Mitch Verde, and Yanping Cui. 2016. "Child-Rearing Practices of the Carrier First Nation in Northern British Columbia." *Canadian Journal of Native Studies* 36 (1): 153–77.

O'Neill, Therese. 2013. "'Don't Think of Ugly People': How Parenting Advice Has Changed." *The Atlantic*, April 19, 2013. https://www.theatlantic.com/health/archive/2013/04/dont-think-of-ugly-people-how-parenting-advice-has-changed/275108/.

O'Reilly, Andrea. 2006. "Between the Baby and the Bathwater: Some Thoughts on a Mother-Centred Theory and Practice of Feminist Mothering." *Journal of the Association for Research on Mothering* 8 (1/2): 323–30. https://jarm.journals.yorku.ca/index.php/jarm/article/view/5036/4230.

———. 2014. "Introduction." In *Mothers, Mothering and Motherhood across Cultural Differences*, edited by Andrea O'Reilly, 1–6. Toronto: Demeter.

Ortner, Sherri. 2016. "Dark Anthropology." *HAU Journal of Ethnographic Theory* 6(1): 47–73. doi/pdfplus/10.14318/hau6.1.004.

Panagopoulou, Efharis, Stan Maes, Bernard Rimé, and Anthony Montgomery. 2006. "Social Sharing of Emotion in Anticipation of Cardiac Surgery: Effects on Preoperative Distress." *Journal of Health Psychology* 11 (5): 809–20. https://doi.org/10.1177%2F1359105306066644.

Parker, Hayley. 2016. "Experiences of Hypochondriasis in Relation to HIV and AIDS: An Autoethnography." In *AIDS Saskatoon: A History of Service, Hope, and Engagement*, edited by Pamela Downe and Rebecca Dravland, 104–16. Saskatoon: AnthroInSight.

Pegoraro, Leonardo. 2015. "Second-Rate Victims: The Forced Sterilization of Indigenous Peoples in the USA and Canada." *Settler Colonial Studies* 5 (2): 161–73. https://doi.org/10.1080/2201473X.2014.955947.

Peters, Evelyn J., and Tyler A. McCreary. 2008. "Poor Neighbourhoods and the Changing Geography of Food Retailing in Saskatoon, 1984–2004." *Canadian Journal of Urban Research* 17 (1): 78–106.

Pink, Sarah. 2012. *Situating Everyday Life*. Thousand Oaks, CA: Sage.

Posadzki, Alexandra. 2013. "Despite Risks, Sedative Called 'Benzos' Widely Used." *Globe and Mail*, July 29, 2013. http://www.theglobeandmail.com/life/health-and-fitness/health/despite-risks-sedatives-called-benzos-widely-used/article13482915/.

Posluns, Michael. 2007. "Congress of Aboriginal Peoples." In *The Canadian Encyclopedia, Historica Canada*. Last edited November 6, 2019. https://www.thecanadianencyclopedia.ca/en/article/congress-of-aboriginal-peoples.

Poudrier, Jennifer, and Roanne Thomas-Maclean. 2009. "'We've Fallen into the Cracks': Aboriginal Women's Experiences with Breast Cancer through Photovoice." *Nursing Inquiry* 16 (4): 306–17. https://doi.org/10.1111/j.1440-1800.2009.00435.x.

Public Health Agency of Canada (PHAC). 2015. *HIV and AIDS in Canada: Surveillance Report to December 31, 2014*. Ottawa: Public Health Agency of Canada and Ministry of Public Works.

———. 2016. *Alcohol Consumption in Canada: The Chief Public Health Officer's Report on the State of Public Health Canada, 2015*. Ottawa: Public Health Agency of Canada.

Racco, Mailisa. 2017. "How Much Does It Cost to Raise a Kid in Canada?" *Global News*, January 12, 2017. http://globalnews.ca/news/3172459/how-much-does-it-cost-to-raise-a-kid-in-canada/.

Raiford, Leigh. 2011. *Imprisoned in a Luminous Glare: Photography and the African American Freedom Struggle*. Durham: University of North Carolina Press.

Reimer, Vanessa, and Sarah Sahagian. 2015. "Contextualizing the Mother-Blame Game." In *The Mother-Blame Game*, edited by Vanessa Reimer and Sarah Sahagian, 1–18. Toronto: Demeter.

Riley, Diana, Ed Sawka, Peter Conley, David Hewitt, Wayne Mitic, Christiane Poulin, Robin Room, et al. 1999. "Harm Reduction: Concepts and Practice." *Substance Use and Misuse* 34 (1): 9–24. https://doi.org/10.3109/10826089909035632.

Roberts, Elizabeth S. 2012. *God's Laboratory: Assisted Reproduction in the Andes*. Berkeley: University of California Press.

Robertson, Leslie. 2007. "Taming Space: Drug Use, HIV, and Homemaking in Downtown Eastside Vancouver." *Gender, Place and Culture* 14 (5): 527–49.

Rodman, Margaret. 1992. "Empowering Place: Multilocality and Multivocality." *American Anthropologist* 94 (3): 640–56. https://doi.org/10.1525/aa.1992.94.3.02a00060.

Rosenblatt, Paul C. 2008. "Grief across Cultures: A Review and Research Agenda." In *Handbook of Bereavement Research and Practice: Advances in Theory and Intervention*, edited by Margaret Stroebe, Robert Hansson, Henk Schut, and Wolfgang Stroebe, 207–22. Washington, DC: American Psychological Association.

Ross, John M. 1994. *What Men Want: Mothers, Fathers, and Manhood*. Boston: Harvard University Press.

Ruby, Jini, Stacey Shaw, Elinor W. Chemonges, and Cole Hooley. 2009. "Changing Patterns of Family Care in Uganda: Father Absence and Patrilineal Neglect in the Face of HIV/AIDS." *Families in Society* 90 (1): 110–18. https://www.researchgate.net/deref/http%3A%2F%2Fdx.doi.org%2F10.1606%2F1044-3894.3852.

Sacket, Walter W. 1962. *Bringing Up Babies: A Family Doctor's Practical Approach to Child Care*. New York: Harper and Row.

Salloum, Alec. 2015. "Rates of HIV Deaths in Saskatchewan." *Regina Leader-Post*, December 15, 2015. http://leaderpost.com/news/local-news/rates-of-hiv-related-deaths-in-saskatchewan-more-than-four-times-national-average.

Sandelowski, Margarete, and Julie Barroso. 2003. "Motherhood in the Context of Maternal HIV Infection." *Research in Nursing & Health* 26 (6): 470–82. https://doi.org/10.1002/nur.10109.

Saskatchewan Ministry of Health. 2010. *HIV and AIDS in Saskatchewan 2009*. Regina: Saskatchewan Ministry of Health.

———. 2018. *HIV and AIDS in Saskatchewan 2017*. Regina: Saskatchewan Ministry of Health.

Sayer, Liana C. 2005. "Gender, Time, and Inequality: Trends in Women's and Men's Paid Work, Unpaid Work, and Free Time." *Social Forces* 84 (1): 285–303. https://doi.org/10.1353/sof.2005.0126.

Scheper-Hughes, Nancy. 1993. *Death without Weeping: The Violence of Everyday Life in Brazil*. Berkeley: University of California Press.

Seligman, Adam B., Rahel R. Wasserfall, and David W. Montgomery. 2015. *Living with Difference: How to Build Community in a Divided World*. Berkeley: University of California Press.

Semley, Lorelle D. 2011. *Mother Is Gold, Father Is Glass: Gender and Colonialism in a Yoruba Town*. Bloomington: University of Indiana Press.

Setel, Philip W. 1999. *A Plague of Paradoxes: AIDS, Culture, and Demography in Northern Tanzania*. Chicago: University of Chicago Press.

Shah, Sonia. 2016. *Pandemic: Tracking Contagion, from Cholera to Ebola and Beyond*. New York: Picador.

Shankar, Arjun. 2016. "Auteurship and Image-Making: A (Gentle) Critique of the Photovoice Method." *Visual Anthropology Review* 32 (2): 157–66. https://doi.org/10.1111/var.12107.

Sharp, Henry. 1979. *Chipewyan Marriage*. Canadian Ethnology Service Paper no. 58. Ottawa: National Museum of Man.

Shepard, Glen. 2002. "Three Days for Weeping: Dreams, Emotions, and Death in the Peruvian Amazon." *Medical Anthropology Quarterly* 16 (2): 200–29. https://doi.org/10.1525/maq.2002.16.2.200.

Shirani, Fiona, Karen Henwood, and Carrie Coltart. 2012. "Meeting the Challenges of Intensive Parenting Culture: Gender, Risk Management and the Moral Parent." *Sociology* 46 (1): 25–40. https://doi.org/10.1177%2F0038038511416169.

Silver, Ellen J., Laurie J. Bauman, Sheila Camacho, and Jan Hudis. 2003. "Factors Associated with Psychological Distress in Urban Mothers with Late Stage HIV/AIDS." *AIDS and Behavior* 7 (4): 421–31. https://doi.org/10.1023/b:aibe.0000004734.21864.25.

Singer, Merrill. 2009. *Introduction to Syndemics: A Critical Systems Approach to Public and Community Health*. San Francisco: Jossey-Bass.

Singer, Merrill, and Scott Clair. 2003. "Syndemics and Public Health: Reconceptualizing Disease in Bio-Social Context." *Medical Anthropology Quarterly* 17 (4): 423–41. https://doi.org/10.1525/maq.2003.17.4.423.

Singer, Merrill, D. Ann Herring, Judith Littleton, and Melanie Rock. 2011. "Syndemics in Global Health." In *A Companion to Medical Anthropology*, edited by Merrill Singer and Pamela I. Erickson, 159–79. Malden, MA: Wiley-Blackwell.

Smith, Dorothy. 1993. "The Standard North American Family." *Journal of Family Issues* 14 (1): 50–65. https://doi.org/10.1177%2F0192513X93014001005.

Smith, James G.E. 1981. "Chipewyan." In *Handbook of North American Indians*, edited by June Helm, 271–84. Washington, DC: Smithsonian Press.

Soloducha, Alex. 2018. "Saskatchewan's HIV Rate Highest in Canada." *CBC News*, October 12, 2017. https://www.cbc.ca/news/canada/saskatchewan/saskatchewan-hiv-rate-highest-canada-1.4351057.

Sowder, Barbara, and Marvin R. Burt. 1980. "Children of Addicts and Non-Addicts." In *Heroin Addicted Parents and Their Children: Two Studies*, edited by the National Institute on Drug Abuse, 19–35. Washington, DC: Department of Health and Human Services.

Smith, Linda Tuhiwai. 1999. *Decolonizing Methodologies: Research and Indigenous Peoples*. London: Zed Books.

Special Advisory Committee on the Epidemic of Opioid Overdoses. 2019. "National Report: Apparent Opioid-Related Deaths in Canada (January 2016 to December 2018)." Ottawa: Public Health Agency of Canada. https://health-infobase.canada.ca/datalab/national-surveillance-opioid-mortality.html.

Spiwak, Rae, Jitender Sareen, Brenda Elias, Patricia Martens, Garry Munro, and James Bolton. 2012. "Complicated Grief in Aboriginal Populations." *Dialogues in Clinical Neuroscience* 14 (2): 204–9. https://www.dialogues-cns.org/contents-14-2/dialoguesclinneurosci-14-204/.

Spock, Benjamin. 1946. *The Common Sense Book of Baby and Child Care*. New York: Duell, Sloan and Pearce.

Statistics Canada. 2017a. "Income Highlight Tables: 2016 Census." https://www12.statcan.gc.ca/census-recensement/2016/dp-pd/hlt-fst/inc-rev/index-eng.cfm.

———. 2017b. *Women in Canada: Women and the Criminal Justice System*. http://www.statcan.gc.ca/daily-quotidien/170606/dq170606a-eng.htm?CMP=mstatcan.

Stearns, Peter. 2009. "Analyzing the Role of Culture in Shaping American Childhood: A Twentieth Century Case." *European Journal of Developmental Psychology* 6 (1): 34–52. https://www.researchgate.net/deref/http%3A%2F%2Fdx.doi.org%2F10.1080%2F17405620802497024.

Stokes, Elizabeth Fairfield. 2014. "I Am a Helicopter Parent – And I Don't Apologize." *Time*, October 21, 2014. https://time.com/3528619/in-defense-of-helicopter-parents/.

Stote, Karen. 2012. "The Coercive Sterilization of Aboriginal Women in Canada." *American Indian Culture and Resource Journal* 36 (3): 117–50. https://doi.org/10.17953/aicr.36.3.7280728r6479j650.

Sutherns, Rebecca, and Ivy Lynn Bourgeault. 2008. "Accessing Maternity Care in Rural Canada: There's More to the Story than Distance to Doctor." *Health Care for Women International* 29 (8/9): 863–83.

Taussig, Michael. 1999. *Defacement: Public Secrecy and the Labor of the Negative*. Stanford, CA: Stanford University Press.

Thurer, Shari L. 1994. *The Myths of Motherhood: How Culture Reinvents the Good Mother*. New York: Penguin.

Tomas, Kristina, P. Dhami, C. Houston, S. Ogunnaike-Cooke, and C. Rank. 2015. "HIV in Canada: 2009–2014." *Canada's Communicable Disease Report* 41 (2): 292–303. https://doi.org/10.14745/ccdr.v41i12a01.

Truth and Reconciliation Commission of Canada (TRC). 2015a. *Honouring the Truth, Reconciling for the Future: Summary of the Final Report of the Truth and Reconciliation Commission of Canada*. Ottawa: TRC.

———. 2015b. *The Survivors Speak: A Report of the Truth and Reconciliation Commission of Canada*. Ottawa: TRC.

United Nations. 2018. "Ending Poverty." https://www.un.org/en/sections/issues-depth/poverty/.

Valdez, Maria. 2001. "A Metaphor for HIV Positive Mexican and Puerto Rican Women." *Western Journal of Nursing Research* 23 (5): 517–35. https://doi.org/10.1177%2F01939450122045357.

Vandenbeld Giles, Melinda. 2012. "From 'Need' to 'Risk': The Neoliberal Construction of the 'Bad' Mother." *Journal of the Motherhood Initiative for Research and Community Involvement* 2 (1): 194–212. https://jarm.journals.yorku.ca/index.php/jarm/article/view/35342/32067.

———. 2014. "Introduction: An Alternative Mother-Centred Economic Paradigm." In *Mothering in the Age of Neoliberalism*, edited by Melinda Vandenbeld Giles, 1–30. Toronto: Demeter.

VanStone, James W. 1963. *The Snowdrift Chipewyan*. Ottawa: Northern Co-ordination and Research Centre, Department of Northern Affairs and National Resources, Government of Canada.

Vasiliki, Douglas. 2013. *Introduction to Aboriginal Health and Health Care in Canada: Bridging Health and Healing*. New York: Springer.

Vescera, Zak. 2019. "Saskatchewan's First Safe Consumption Site Aims to Foster Community." *Saskatoon Star Phoenix*, November 5, 2019. https://thestarphoenix.com/news/local-news/saskatchewans-first-safe-consumption-site-aims-to-foster-community.

Vincent, Carole. 2013. *Why Do Women Earn Less than Men? A Synthesis of Findings from Canadian Microdata*. Ottawa: Statistics Canada and the Canadian Research Data Network Centre.

Vogel, Lauren. 2015. "HIV in Saskatchewan Merits Urgent Response." *Canadian Medical Association Journal* 187 (11): 793–94. https://dx.doi.org/10.1503%2Fcmaj.109-5105.

Waiser, Bill. 2005. *Saskatchewan: A New History*. Calgary: Fitzhenry and Whiteside.

Waldram, James B. 1997. *The Way of the Pipe: Aboriginal Spirituality and Symbolic Healing in Canadian Prisons*. Peterborough, ON: Broadview.

———. 2004. *Revenge of the Windigo: The Constructions of the Mind and Mental Health of North American Aboriginal Peoples*. Toronto: University of Toronto Press.

Warren, Jeremy. 2012a. "Needle Exchange Debated." *Saskatoon Star Phoenix*, June 22, 2012, A3.

———. 2012b. "33rd Street Neighbours Debate Needle Exchange." *Saskatoon Star Phoenix*, June 21, 2012, B7.

Warry, Wayne. 1998. *Unfinished Dreams: Community Healing and the Reality of Aboriginal Self-Government*. Toronto: University of Toronto Press.

Watson, John B., and Rosalie Watson. 1928. *Psychological Care of Infant and Child*. New York: W.W. Norton.
Weeks, Carly, and Karen Howlett. 2016. "Prescriptions of Opioid Drugs Skyrocketing in Canada." *Globe and Mail*, April 5, 2016. http://www.theglobeandmail.com/life/health-and-fitness/health/despite-risks-sedatives-called-benzos-widely-used/article13482915/.
Wierzbicka, Anna. 2004. "Emotion and Culture: Arguing with Martha Nussbaum." *Ethos* 31 (4): 577–600. https://doi.org/10.1525/eth.2003.31.4.577.
Williams, Rhaisa Kameda. 2016. "Towards a Theorization of Black Maternal Grief." *Transforming Anthropology* 24 (1): 17–30. https://doi.org/10.1111/traa.12057.
Wilson, Kathy, Judith MacIntosh, and Grace Getty. 2007. "'Tapping a Tie': Successful Partnerships in Managing Addictions with Methadone." *Issues in Mental Health Nursing* 28 (9): 977–96. https://www.researchgate.net/deref/http%3A%2F%2Fdx.doi.org%2F10.1080%2F01612840701522176.
Wolf, Joan B. 2011. *Is Breast Best? Taking on the Breastfeeding Experts and the New High Stakes of Motherhood*. New York: New York University Press.
———. 2016. "Framing Mothers: Childcare Research and the Normalization of Maternal Care." *Signs* 41 (3): 627–51. https://www.researchgate.net/deref/http%3A%2F%2Fdx.doi.org%2F10.1086%2F684240.
World Health Organization. 2014. "World AIDS Day: Business Unusual: Time to End the AIDS Epidemic." http://www.who.int/woman_child_accountability/ierg/news/ierg_statement_AIDS_1_december_2014/en/.
Younging, Gregory. 2018. *Elements of Indigenous Style: A Guide for Writing by and about Indigenous Peoples*. Toronto: Brush Education.

Index

TC TEACHING CULTURE

Ethnographies for the Classroom

Editor: John Barker, University of British Columbia

This series is an essential resource for instructors searching for ethnographic case studies that are contemporary, engaging, provocative, and created specifically with undergraduate students in mind. Written with clarity and personal warmth, books in the series introduce students to the core methods and orienting frameworks of ethnographic research and provide a compelling entry point to some of the most urgent issues faced by people around the globe today.

Recent Books in the Series

Collective Care: Indigenous Motherhood, Family, and HIV/AIDS by Pamela J. Downe (2021)

I Was Never Alone, or Oporniki: An Ethnographic Play on Disability in Russia by Cassandra Hartblay (2020)

Millennial Movements: Positive Social Change in Urban Costa Rica by Karen Stocker (2020)

From Water to Wine: Becoming Middle Class in Angola by Jess Auerbach (2020)

Deeply Rooted in the Present: Heritage, Memory, and Identity in Brazilian Quilombos by Mary Lorena Kenny (2018)

Long Night at the Vepsian Museum: The Forest Folk of Northern Russia and the Struggle for Cultural Survival by Veronica Davidov (2017)

Truth and Indignation: Canada's Truth and Reconciliation Commission on Indian Residential Schools, second edition, by Ronald Niezen (2017)

Merchants in the City of Art: Work, Identity, and Change in a Florentine Neighborhood by Anne Schiller (2016)

Ancestral Lines: The Maisin of Papua New Guinea and the Fate of the Rainforest, second edition, by John Barker (2016)

Love Stories: Language, Private Love, and Public Romance in Georgia by Paul Manning (2015)

Culturing Bioscience: A Case Study in the Anthropology of Science by Udo Krautwurst (2014)

Fields of Play: An Ethnography of Children's Sports by Noel Dyck (2012)

Made in Madagascar: Sapphires, Ecotourism, and the Global Bazaar by Andrew Walsh (2012)

Red Flags and Lace Coiffes: Identity and Survival in a Breton Village by Charles R. Menzies (2011)
Rites of the Republic: Citizens' Theatre and the Politics of Culture in Southern France by Mark Ingram (2011)